Your Psychic World A-Z

Tara Bonewitz, who writes under the name Ann Petrie, is a spiritual teacher and counsellor as well as a popular astrologer. She has written three astrology books, including *SUN SIGNS, YOUR KIND OF LOVING*, and *YOUR PSYCHIC WORLD*, which will be followed by *LET YOUR HEART RE-MEMBER*, about reincarnation and spiritual law.

Tara broadasts and writes on astrological, psychic and spiritual subjects. As a counsellor she teaches meditation, mediumistic techniques and self-healing, and specialises in recall of past lives to cure phobias and show direction in life.

Together with her husband Ra, author of *COSMIC CRYSTALS*, she gives workshops on crystal energies worldwide. Tara's part of the workshop has always involved past-life memories, healing and meditation.

If you feel you need help with a specific problem, please write enclosing a stamped addressed envelope to: 10 South Molton Street, W1, and Tara will put you in touch with a counsellor or healer she has trained.

Ann Petrie

Your Psychic World A-Z

An Everyday Guide

ARROW BOOKS

Arrow Books Limited
17–21 Conway Street, London W1P 6JD

An imprint of the Hutchinson Publishing Group

London Melbourne Sydney Auckland
Johannesburg and agencies throughout
the world

First published by Arrow 1984

© Ann Petrie 1984

Set in Linotron Baskerville
by Book Economy Services, Burgess Hill, Sussex

Printed and bound in Great Britain
by Anchor Brendon Limited, Tiptree, Essex

ISBN 0 09 939450 2

I dedicate this book to
all those of the White Brotherhood
who have helped me find out who and what I am,
those in spirit and those on the earth,
but especially to Ra
whom I love.

Contents

Introduction

You were born to learn how to love. That is the lesson of planet Earth. You were also born to find out who and what you are because, in order to love others, you need to accept and love yourself.

From the moment you were born, immense influences shaped the way you thought, what you believed, and how you expressed those beliefs. Sooner or later, however, you are bound to question it all. Books you've read, the conversations you've had, the groups you've been to see, the churches you've attended, the beliefs of your parents and your friends, the programmes you have watched on television or listened to on the radio, the stories in the newspapers and magazines. Sooner or later, you will ask yourself, what is it all about? What am I doing here and what is my purpose? And, finally, you'll ask yourself, what is really true and what is truth?

Since you were born you've been searching for that truth out of all that mumbo-jumbo, the half truths, innuendos and lies. That truth is a thin gold thread that needs to be picked up and gathered into yourself, for once you are on the path of truth you will never move off it.

Your Psychic World looks at the ideas and practices from the past, some of which may shock and surprise you and some of which will show great beauty, harmony and understanding. The teachings of the masters, throughout time, apply today as much as yesterday, for the same fundamental lessons have to be learnt and often the same patterns repeated. All that has happened is that the physical world has slightly changed and the fight for survival, for most people, is not so intense.

Today we think we can control everything, but this is a great illusion. By cutting ourselves off from the forces of nature, we lose out all down the line. Remember, too, that although some of the things talked about in *Your Psychic World* may seem mumbo-jumbo, it is us who have created them at some time or another. They are part of what we have done.

The ideas of thousands of years ago are the same, but the way they are presented has changed. What was considered magic yesterday is now thought of as science. What was considered as heretic practice or witchcraft is now a normal style of living. You need to consider the time-frame around many of the events and ideas described, for political and physical forces shaped our thinking and feeling. When we were struggling to find enough to eat our reliance on the nature spirits and the elements was vital and their cooperation was part of daily life, as well as part of magical practice.

The idea of this book came because so many people wrote to me, through my astrology columns, at great length about their problems, their hopes, their doubts and anxieties but, above all, their fears. Fear of living and fear of dying, fear of being lonely, fear of not being loved, fear of not having enough money, fear of fear. All the people that have ever written to me were searching, to find out who and what they are. What was the meaning of it all? What was the purpose of pain, sorrow or loss? The dreams and the nightmares? The feeling of being loved or the feeling of being cursed? I could feel the anguish through the lines written on the sheets of paper and I could almost see their eyes often dulled with pain. So here is the book I hope will provide you with the thread of truth that you need to change things in your life. Grasp that thread and pull it to yourself as I have done, and your life literally becomes a miracle. Flowing with the way things are instead of the way you demand them to be is a wonderful way of being. You don't stand alone. You have never stood alone. God within us makes us all one and those who look after us in the spirit world give us the richness of the tapestry. Unfolding your true potential is like the unfolding of a flower, a perfect and holy miracle. This is your birthright. I hope I will touch your feelings with these words and touch your heart.

I am grateful for this opportunity

My love to you

Ann Petrie

London 1984

Adept

Someone who has reached a certain degree of clarity and knowledge about the nature and laws of the universe is termed an adept. This is usually an old 'soul' who has spent many lives on the earth, perfecting abilities, and will be known as an initiate or master. Adepts can take to the left or the right path, the positive or the negative, and I have met several of both. What is impressive is that an adept is very seldom agitated or perturbed by anything, knowing how and when to use emotions to best effect. The positive adept operates from the heart centre and not from the head, and flows with life rather than trying to manipulate it for his own ends. No longer influenced by the desires of the world, the adept is both intensely human and completely in touch with the spiritual self. Certainly the adept will accept that:

All the world's a stage,
And all the men and women merely players:
They have their exits and their entrances;
And one man in his time plays many parts.

William Shakespeare
As You Like It II, vii

Affirmation

An affirmation is something that is said over and over again, and is a form of auto-suggestion, rather like hypnosis. It is very easy to do and can be very beneficial if you use it sensibly. It takes the mind twenty-one days to absorb anything new, so an affirmation will not work in twenty days or even nineteen days. Think what you would like to change in your life. Are you happy with your figure, or would you like to have a slimmer, more vital body, or perhaps you want to give up smoking once and for all? Let's say that you wish to give up smoking; first, you work out a statement to the effect that you do not wish to smoke or that you will lose the desire to smoke. Be careful in your exact wording because, if you say something like, 'I will never smoke again,' this is far more aggressive than a suggestion. It is not as acceptable as, 'I will have no desire to smoke.' Work this out with care for you must repeat the statement two or three times a day. Besides affirming the statement for twenty-one days or more, its effectiveness will depend on your ability to feed your mind. Most problems respond to this auto-suggestion technique, and you may remember that, as a child, you were probably taught to say, 'I am getting better and better every day,' at least I was. 'Better at what' was never defined; it probably meant good and quiet! A popular form of auto-suggestion is the use of rosary beads. This is an affirmation, in itself, for each bead represents a wish or a statement and can be used, for example, to the effect of wanting to become a more positive person. When you pass the beads through your fingers you repeat the statement in your mind, silently or out loud, and this will help to feed the subconscious mind with your wish of intention.

Is is important to choose words which bring a flash of the fulfillment of the demand. For instance, if you have an empty purse or wallet, imagine it crammed full of notes of every value, crammed so full that you can hardly shut it without an effort. An affirmation for this could be, 'My supply is endless and immediate, abundance is my right.' Choose the affirmation that appeals to you most and simply use it over and over again; wave it over the situation which confronts you. A lovely one is, 'I love everyone and everyone loves me. I am at peace with myself and the whole world.'

Any technique of auto-suggestion will be more effective if you use it just before you go to sleep. This is due to the fact that the unconscious mind is much easier to reach in a relaxed state. The whole process of auto-suggestion must be methodical and you should repeat the same statement of your intention over a period of time. Don't chop and change; it will not work. Remember, though, that the mind is a very powerful tool and you should be careful that you are using that tool properly, so personal difficulties do need to be looked at closely and you are the only one who will know whether you are just hiding these things or dealing with them. Auto-suggestion should always be directed at helping you to see and understand the area that you want to change within yourself. The whole approach to it should be done in a very gentle manner so that you gradually build up confidence within yourself and always feel comfortable with the effect that the affirmation is having.

I can, from personal experience, say that affirmations work as I did this myself for a period of six months when I wanted to lose a great deal of weight. I specified how much weight I wanted to lose each month and the weight simply dropped off. It is strange how these things work, but they do work and are worth persevering with.

Akashic Record

Akashic is a Sanskrit word which means fundamental, etheric substance of the universe. The Akashic Record is the record or book of all the thoughts and feelings you and everyone else have had on the earth. These books are often called the Universal Memory of Nature, and everyone has the inherent ability to see his own book. It is simply a matter of developing the ability and this means getting in tune with yourself first! For only when your spiritual and mental powers are developed sufficiently can you go and see your own book and find out what lives you have led, and everything you have felt, thought or done on the earth. The books are kept in a type of British Museum in the sky. You are greeted at the door by the doorkeeper and you need to ask the doorkeeper to show you your particular book. It may be in the form of a scroll, a tablet, a parchment or a bound book. If you have the ability you'll be able to find out all about yourself as the need arises. The books are kept in a temple or library. Rows and rows of them, line upon line, stack upon stack, corridor upon corridor. Any good psychic can tell your previous lives by going to these records which exist in the etheric plane where everything is electromagnetic vibration. It's quite a trip, believe me, and one that is never forgotten. Not only can you recognize the person from the cover of the book but you can also read the true spiritual name on the cover. Some books I have seen are charred and turned up at the edges and blackened as if they have been pulled out of a fire. Others are beautifully illuminated scrolls, and others are embossed with gold leaf and mother-of-pearl with pages in rainbow colours. Yet others are bound in red leather with special emblems and powerful symbols. Some are scrolls, rolled up and stored in a jar, and others are kept on shelves or in alcoves.

Alchemy

Alchemists don't pop up at every street corner today but the art or science of alchemy has been around for thousands of years, and the stories and legends about it will continue. An alchemist is often depicted as muttering strange incantations and stirring a bubbling concoction of base metal on a fire, hoping it will turn into gold. Not all alchemists were, of course, like this, and some of the world's best minds during the last twenty centuries have pitted their wits to harness the secrets of nature. Alchemy probably started in ancient Egypt when the goldsmiths experimented with alloys and in Greece where philosophers tried to fathom the mystery of the elements, Earth, Air, Fire and Water. Alchemists tried to rearrange and transmute matter from one form to the other, and although their basic aim was to transmute the base metal into gold the higher goal was to achieve spiritual and physical immortality.

The idea of being able to turn base metals into gold, or finding the El of Life, has always appealed to man's imagination. Today there are very few practising alchemists but the stories and legends of their work continue. The fact is that scientists have discovered how to change base metals into gold but the process is uneconomical. The teachings of alchemy were based on the idea that man not only had a physical body but also had a spirit or soul. They took this idea a little further and saw that the body, or matter, of the world was not only alive, but was also infused with spirit. They felt that they only had to compress or concentrate this spirit and they would discover the secret of how to change one aspect of nature into a different aspect. This illusive catalyst is known as the Philosophers Stone; this was not so much a solid stone as a powder or liquid that could be added to base metals such as mercury or lead, and turn them into gold.

The substance called the Philosophers Stone is also known as the El or Universal Panacea. When this substance is swallowed it is supposed to give you everlasting life. There is a legend in China that tells of a great master called Wei Po Yung who found, and took, the El with his disciple; unfortunately, his little dog accidentally ate what was left of the El. Presumbably they all found everlasting life and are still taking the dog for a walk! There is another story of a seventeenth-century chemist who claimed he had the vital constituent of the El in the waters of a mineral spring. This substance has since been identified as sodium sulphate, used today as a laxative.

The alchemists' experiments were very primitive and resulted in many disastrous explosions. Their studies of minerals, plants and elements were quite extensive, but their records are laden with obscure symbols and codes due to their work being considered heresy; also they had to prevent the uninitiated from delving into their secrets.

The whole issue of alchemy has got such a bad name because there were so many fraudulent attempts by alchemists to become famous. Even as late as 1782 a chemist called John Price claimed he had turned mercury into gold. When he was asked by the Royal Society to perform the experiment in public he reluctantly agreed. On the day of the experiment he drank some poison and died in front of the invited audience.

The more serious aspects of alchemy show that alchemists investigated how man as a spiritual being can perfect every aspect of himself and change from being earth-bound to being highly spiritual. The symbolism of turning the base metal into gold may represent exactly what the real alchemist was trying to do within himself. Maybe the alchemist was taking a more scientific approach to the age-old problem of 'Know thyself.' Among the great alchemists were the Count de St Germain, Isaac Newton and Roger Bacon.

My husband and a close friend were both alchemists in seventeenth-century Germany, in a past life, and remember well working very hard indeed to turn base metal into gold. Neither succeeded though they did get involved with spiritual and universal laws, gaining a great deal of understanding and knowledge. Both were also regarded with intense suspicion and died premature deaths. Alchemy today is very much on the spiritual level, especially as it has been proved that base metal can be turned into gold. Today we seek the spiritual level of alchemy and not its practicalities or material benefits.

Amulets and Talismans

The difference between an amulet and a talisman is that the amulet is usually worn as a charm, often in the form of jewellery, while a talisman does not necessarily need to be worn; unlike an amulet it always incorporates symbols to represent a force or forces being called upon to gain a particular end.

In Egyptian times every man, woman and child wore at least one amulet or charm and some of these took the form of exquisite jewellery. They were seen as power symbols and in the mummy wrappings of Tutankhamen 150 amulets were found. The most powerful Egyptian amulet was considered to be the scarab, the symbol of life dedicated to Ra, the Sun God. In burial rites the scarab was used to replace the heart and had a magical spell carved on its back requesting immortality! The eye of Horus and the buckle of Isis were other powerful amulets, usually to protect the wearer from the evil eye. The Ankh, a cross with a ringed head, also represented life and immortality. In Moslem countries another amulet is the hand of Fatima, supposed to protect its owner from harm.

Certain symbols have certain attributes. The most common ones are the crescent moon for protection and personal and material advancement, the heart for protection and true love, the horseshoe for prestige and good fortune, a key for liberation, knowledge and initiation. A knot means protection and true love, while an owl signifies wisdom and knowledge; a serpent is a symbol for eternity and divine power, giving vitality and longevity. Other symbols that are commonly worn are Solomon's Seal, a symbol of interlaced triangles which protects against all harm and is thought to be all-powerful, and the Tau, the 'T' cross, which represents purity of thought and is said to promote good health.

Amulets have been used since earliest times and are usually an object such as a bracelet, brooch, medallion, necklace or pendant, ring or seal that's worn on the person or carried close to it. The St Christopher is one of the commonest amulets today and is found on key rings, pendants and also swinging from mirrors in motor cars. St Christopher is, of course, the saint who is said to protect travellers. An amulet doesn't have to be made of metal but can be a rabbit's foot, or a crystal or a pebble of unusual shape or colour. Even gamblers have lucky coins! An amulet is often regarded as a 'lucky' protective device and is said to be a safeguard against accidents, ill-luck, misfortune and evil. People tend to wear amulets if they're faced with a stressful or difficult condition and also if they feel they're going into danger. I myself wore an Egyptian-symbol charm bracelet for many years simply because I felt attached to it. No doubt this was a memory from a previous existence! Amulets can also have signs, symbols or words of power engraved on them and even spells. If you believe that the amulet can help you then it can probably do so, but if you don't believe it, then, for you, it's a nice piece of jewellery or keepsake.

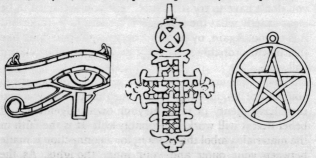

Talismans have been used as protective devices against evil for a very long time, although they can, of course, be used for exactly the opposite. Anything can be a talisman, but it is usually a stone, a pendant or a ring which has been charged with magical power. Usually, the talisman is something that is engraved and can have a magic square of either numbers or letters. It is like a charm except that it is always prepared ritually by someone who practises magic, in order to achieve a specific result. You may need a talisman, for instance, for protection, for being more positive or to heal yourself. Or you could wear one to help with a health problem, a problem with your love life or even a bereavement or illness. Talismans can also be prepared from wood, parchment or even leaves and often they are buried or destroyed as part of the ritual. Unfortunately, like most things, they can be used for positive or negative purposes though mostly they are a protective device for warding off evil. The Eye of Horus or the Eye of Ra are also effective for doing this. I often wear the Chinese symbol for happiness as a talisman simply because it gives me pleasure and makes me feel better. Perhaps you have something similar?

Talismatic magic requires specialized knowledge and is a mixture of occultism and astrology. A talisman is engraved or inscribed with suitable symbols and colours. There are plenty of people who advertise talismans, so you don't have to try it yourself, but you will need to be clear exactly what the talisman is for and how important it is to you. Again, by putting energy into something like this it will probably work very much as a lucky charm will work.

How do talismans work? If you give a lot of thought to your choice of talisman and find one that pleases you and then have plenty of faith in your own judgement and belief that it will work, it probably will. It is the faith in the material symbol that does it, for a connection is made between your outer and your inner thoughts. As the energy flows between the two you allow whatever it is you want to happen – to happen.

Angels

Angels are not found only in the Bible for most people feel that they have a guardian angel looking after them, and take a great deal of comfort in that thought. Angels appear in the Bible the whole time and are seen as missionaries from another world. It was the angel within the pillar, that led the Israelites for forty years as they wandered in the wilderness, that gave religious guidance to Moses and provided him with the Ten Commandments. Jacob also talked with angels and Jesus taught that angels are very concerned with the success of their mission of earth. Yet, what are they? They are certainly not human but supernatural beings with kindly qualities who, by their own gentleness and unassuming manner, are an example of goodness. Beings of pure spirit and figures of light formed by the element of Fire, their assistance in our everyday affairs provides the divine intervention that gives hope in times of need. It is certainly comforting to know that, when trouble strikes or there is a heavy problem to think over, help is there at some level. The messengers of God do not come only when there are great events, such as the announcement of the birth of Jesus, but are there for the smallest details of our everyday lives. They provide a communication network and link the world of spirit to the world of earth; they also provide a wealth of knowledge and information, if only your heart and mind is open to this possibility. When you're meditating or helping to heal someone, then the angelic energy is very close to you and the kindness and gentleness can be felt.

Gabriel, which means 'God is my strength', is one of the higher ranking angels of Judaeo-Christian and Mohammedan religious law. He is the angel of annunciation, resurrection, mercy, vengeance, death and revelation. Apart from Michael he is the only angel mentioned in the Old Testament.

Mohammed claimed it was Gabriel who dictated to

him the Koran, and therefore he is the spirit of truth. According to Jewish legend it was Gabriel who brought about the destruction of the evil cities of Sodom and Gommorah; and, in more recent times, according to the court testimony of Joan of Arc, it was Gabriel who inspired her to go to the succour of the King of France.

Not all of our angels are angelic. Lucifer, often called Satan, is an example of one of the angels that has fallen from grace. Lucifer was supposed to be the most beautiful and gracious being in all of heaven, and he soon became the favourite of the Deity. His beauty and power eventually made him so proud that he began to take over direction of the Universal Plan. The archangel Michael defeated Lucifer in battle and cast him out of the heavenly regions. This occurrence did not please God and it is hoped that some day Lucifer will understand his folly and release himself of his pride. When he does this he can be invited back into the heavenly regions, just like the prodigal son. So remember this when it appears that you have done everything wrong and have hurt everyone around you, because your guardian angel will still be with you and it will depend on your humility whether you will be able to ask for assistance.

An angelic prayer I like is:

Matthew, Mark, Luke and John,
Bless this bed that I lie on.
May four angels guard my bed,
Two at the foot and two at the head,
One to watch and one to pray,
And one to bear my Soul away.

Animal Power

Are animals clairvoyant and can they communicate telepathically? Do they possess special powers that enable them to sense danger? The answer is undoubtedly, 'Yes, they do.' Stories occur frequently in newspapers about the tremendous courage and devotion of dogs and cats that get lost and then find their way home again. Their perseverance against all odds is overwhelming and there are many stories of cats covering 300 miles and even of dogs who have travelled as much as 3000 miles to get back to their beloved owners. This remarkable homing behaviour leads to extraordinary feats, crossing rivers, mountains and even deserts in order to complete their journey. Is this ability extra-sensory perception or something else? It is certainly an ability to communicate between an animal and its environment or indeed the animal and another person. Lots of experiments have been done with various animals over the last few years and their is no doubt that super animals do exist. Dogs have been trained to tap their paws into their owners' hands and to respond to Zener cards (a standard ESP testing tool). It has been found that 70 per cent of the answers are correct; on one occasion the odds against performance by chance were estimated as high as one thousand million to one. There is no doubt that animals do possess senses that we don't or that, in humans, are underdeveloped. Pigeons have tremendously strong homing instincts while bats use echo-location to find out where they are. Horses also have highly developed instincts and sensitivity and are able to find their way back home easily.

It has been known for some time that animals can predict danger through their innate sensitivity, and this includes natural disasters such as avalanches, cyclones and earthquakes. So do animals experience precognition? There is no doubt that, when an earthquake is imminent, dogs bark, rats leave buildings and birds squawk. This was especially apparent in 1963 when an earthquake devastated Skopje in Yugoslavia. Lions and tigers roared in the zoo and other animals simply went berserk, desperately trying to get away. During the

Second World War there were several stories of animals giving an advance warning of bomb raids by causing a commotion.

My own animals are very special indeed, and even as I turn the corner into my street the dogs will bark and the cats go and sit by the front door. This is before I have even got within a hundred yards of the house. They always seem to know which taxi I am in, and although a lot of taxis go up and down the street in Chelsea, they instinctively know when to set up a welcome.

My senior dog who is called Senge-tru is a Lhasa Apso and was wonderfully helpful when I was developing clairvoyance. Since I was a small child I had had no trouble communicating with guides and loved ones who had died, but I couldn't always see them. This wonderful little dog used to rush up to an entity and rush back again and make a great deal of fuss until I acknowledged that someone was in the room. 'Speak up,' I'd say, for then I was on my own and knew what I was doing! Since my sight has developed he has become somewhat redundant, although his appraisal of other people is quite extraordinary. As people arrive for counselling sessions this dog will sit in front of them and literally check them out by looking all over their aura from top to bottom. This is quite an obvious scanning and puts many people off but the dog will then move forward as a friend or will remain firmly where he is. Our Siamese cats are also highly intelligent and sensitive to energies. During meditation all four animals will simply go out of the body and go to sleep. It never fails. During one meditation a very sceptical friend, Stephen, said that the dogs weren't that sensitive yet when we started meditation with him Senge-tru was crunching on a bone and making a great deal of noise. I was in two minds whether to get up and put him out but while I was debating what to do the crunching got slower and slower and quieter and quieter until eventually he fell asleep with the bone still in his mouth. At the end of the meditation he started up again very gradually until the crunching again became quite loud. It was an extraordinary performance and it happened many, many times. Stephen is no longer sceptical! I was told early on that if we have the animals in the room it was often kinder that they went to sleep and went out of the body as the energies could be a little too much for them. As they have been with us quite a while now this doesn't seem to be such a problem even though they normally end up asleep.

Is there an animal heaven? The answer to this is definitely 'Yes' again. A most beautiful cocker spaniel of mine, called Maximillian, died by inadvertently eating poison and his death was very sudden and traumatic. I was really upset by this as he was a much loved dog. Some days later his head and ears appeared to me and I knew that he was not unhappy. Since that time he has popped up from the other side at regular intervals and it is a tremendous feeling of love and communication. Tonie, who lost a beloved cat many years ago, often finds the cat comes and sits on the end of the bed just like she used to. There is even an indentation as the cat makes itself comfortable by its habitual turning round and round before it flops down. I'm sure you have had other experiences with pets that you have loved.

Strange and mysterious stories of dragons, snakes, sea serpents and unicorns still linger among superstitions and fairy tales today. Ever since the serpent tempted Eve in the Garden of Eden and St George killed the Dragon, we have viewed mythical animals with a certain suspiciousness, yet in other cults the serpent is worshipped as a symbol of wisdom and knowledge; the Snake Goddess is alive and well today, especially in Hindu tradition. Each year the local people in southern India find the biggest cobras they can and take them back to the village and worship them as living gods. The sea serpent in Loch Ness is regarded by some as a supernatural entity. In the early Christian teaching, the Devil or Satan in snake form was allegedly fought by the

Christian St Michael in the form of a dragon.

Animals have always been associated with magic because it has always been seen that they have supernatural qualities. Religion and occultists have borrowed heavily on the animal world for they know that the qualities and energies of animals represent power, and that power can be utilized to gain favour with their respective deities. Even today there are many places in the world that still sacrifice animals as part of their ceremony.

The animal's supernatural powers have other uses and there are many cases of a distinct change in an animal's behaviour due to its ability to forsee a calamity about to befall a household or a person. If we have pets, we know sometimes that they seem to know what we are thinking and at other times they seem to be telling us something. Animals do seem to have the quality of spirit and intelligence that we possess and are certainly man's closest allies. We should never forget that we are more animal than human, and it is only when we learn to respect every aspect of life that we may become beings with a human nature.

Astral Body

We all have more than one body! Yes, it's true. The astral body is only one of the subtle bodies that can be seen by a sensitive. Besides your physical body, you have an astral body, etheric body and spiritual body. These are the subtle bodies and take the same shape as the physical but can only be seen by a sensitive, although they can be felt by you. Every night we use the astral body, the soul simply is transferred there while the physical body rests. It is the same when we die for the soul does exactly the same except that the transfer becomes permanent as the cord between the astral body and the physical body slowly dissolves. This can take about three days. At night time, however, which I often think of as the 'little death', the astral body containing the soul is firmly linked to the physical body at all times, and you are often acutely aware of this if you are woken very suddenly by loud noise or by someone shaking you. You are propelled back into the physical body with such force that you often feel disorientated and find that you cannot get your head together. It is when the subtle bodies are out of line that this feeling occurs and the best remedy is to simply lie down again and try to go to sleep and come back naturally. There is absolutely no danger connected with astral projection whether you try to do it in a conscious manner or not.

Occasionally, people remember standing at the end of their beds in one body and looking back and seeing the other quite undisturbed on the bed. This can cause some trauma but it is a perfectly natural thing and may happen every night to everybody. It is the lucky ones who can perceive this. One very common type of projection is to think hard about a place you would wish to go to before you go to sleep, and to concentrate intensely on going there. You may well find that you dream of this place but, instead of dreaming as an observer, you are there taking part in some scenario. You have, literally, astrally projected!

My first conscious astral projection came when I was recovering from a broken rib, and I could hear very heavy breathing in the bed in front of me. I was curious about this for I knew in my mind that I was alone in the bed and in the room, but the breathing seemed particularly laboured and seemed to fill my whole consciousness. I then realized that I was in my astral body outside my physical body and was in my 'double'. I could hear the labouring of the physical body in a way that I don't experience when I'm actually in it, and it seemed that I had an enormous number of tubes in the lungs that made a tremendous racket. After a while I ventured to move to see if the experience stayed with me and it did. I did feel distinctly separate and was able to move apart from the physical body for some distance. I am sure this can happen when you are given drugs after an operation or have an accident.

A friend of mine had a motor-bike accident and as a sensitive was expecting to see his life flash before his eyes. This at least would indicate whether he was alive or dead! As his life didn't appear in this way, he realized he was looking down upon his body, having projected into the astral body on impact. The cord was still firmly attached, however, and within a few minutes he was back in the physical body, unfortunately feeling the consequences of lots of bruises and shock. Your own experiences may be worth recording and you could find plenty of answers to questions that have been bothering you through knowing that you *have* subtle bodies and can operate in them from time to time. This is absolutely natural and part of living.

Astral Projection

This has partly been described in the section on astral body (above), but I would add that the astral body does not necessarily stay on the earth plane, but can move into the astral plane which is another plane of existence altogether. Here, in the astral plane, you can meet those who are physically dead and those who are still in the physical body and communicate with them quite easily. If you really desire to speak to somebody and make contact with them you can achieve this by will, although you may not remember the conversation afterwards, only the feeling. When you are still in the physical environment you'll find that your astral body can walk through walls with ease, and this is an extraordinarily light tingling feeling. If you are projecting voluntarily you can travel anywhere instantly by the sheer force of your will, and you also have the ability to move backwards and forwards in time. Just imagine how useful this can be! The problem is remembering where you have been and what you have done but memory can be improved through training.

You can will yourself to astrally project by simply imagining your spirit body rising off the bed, either horizontally or coming up and standing with the feet on the floor. This is done by the power of visualization, by simply willing it mentally to happen for you. All of a sudden you may find yourself standing up with a tremendous feeling of lightness and freedom, and when you look around you will see that you are attached to your physical body by a thin silver cord. Sometimes, you're aware that the soul simply rises out of the body and floats and soars in the astral world without any conscious visualization or effort. The thin silver cord is always attached to you, so there is no danger that you'll become lost or detached from the body for the cord only breaks when the body can no longer sustain the life force. Dying is the same as astral projection but there is no body to return to. In the astral world you can go anywhere you feel like and meet all kinds of other souls.

Unfortunately, when you return to your body and wake up, you don't often remember where you've been. It often feels as if you've been dreaming except, with astral projection, you are actually involved in the event. Not all astral projection happens when you're asleep or even lying down. I had a wonderful experience of a musician projecting to me quite recently when I was struggling to play 'Clair de Lune' by Debussy on the piano. In spite of intense practice I always went wrong at the same place, and I so wanted to play it really, really well. After a moment's thought, I wondered if I could use my abilities to ask someone to give me some help. I was immediately asked, who did I wish to help me? I replied, 'The best.' A very prominent pianist was instantly by my side and, having introduced himself, sat down in the chair next to me while I started again. I

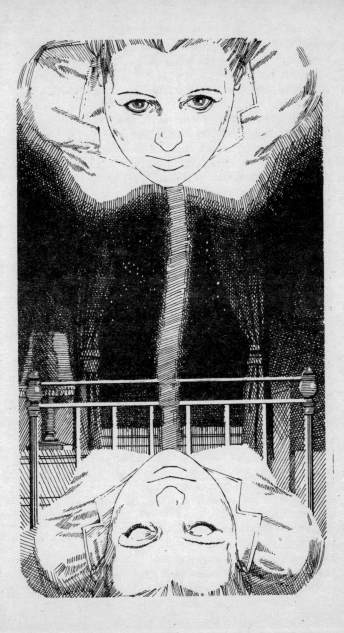

found this very embarrassing and said so, so he simply merged into me and I saw his hands over my hands as I started to play. I have never played like that, to this day, so totally and absolutely wonderfully perfect. And no one, beside myself, heard!

I had an earlier experience when I was eight years old. My beloved grandfather Henry had just died a sudden and unexpected death and I was staying in my grandmother's house, as my mother was ill in hospital. I didn't understand that grandfather Henry had died as no one told me. I simply thought he had gone away and felt very rejected both from that and from the absence of my mother. I was obviously a prime case for a bit of cheering up! I really did feel that no one loved me. That night, just before I went to sleep, I astrally projected into my grandmother's bedroom and went to a very large, old wardrobe. I opened the doors and walked straight through it into the most lovely nursery, full of toys and sunshine. There was a huge rocking horse, a huge teddy bear, lots of dolls to play with and a tremendous feeling of love and caring. There was a lightness about the whole thing and it was truly magical. The next day I jumped up and rushed to the outside of the house. I knew where the bedroom was and I knew this secret room had to be the other side of the wardrobe. The other side of the wardrobe was, however, the outside wall of the house. Yet I could see this room so clearly and I couldn't find it and I wanted to find it so very, very much! This was, of course, grandfather Henry doing his best to cheer me up by creating the sort of room he knew I would have loved. I spent many puzzling hours walking round the house, going in and out of the wardrobe, becoming more and more confused.

Jenny's experience was as follows:

I was seventeen years old, sitting in the choir stalls on a Sunday evening singing in the church choir when I was in college and there was this magical feeling of hush and peace and quiet. The world was at peace and I was kneeling down in the pew with my head resting on my hands feeling very at peace with the world because I loved the evensong service in college, when suddenly I realized I was looking down at everybody from high up in the dome of the church. I was so surprised to be there. I turned round, had a good look at the front, the back and the choir of the church. I looked at myself and I could see every detail of the back of my head resting on my hands. I was wearing a blue nylon dress and I can still see the curve it made on my shoulders. It was a cut-away dress. The church was in darkness and the body of the church was in prayer. The priest was up at the altar and the altar lights were the only ones on. Suddenly I realized that I was right up in the dome of the church, looking down at my body and it was at that point I got frightened and as soon as I was frightened I zoomed back into my body. I was frightened because I thought I was dead. I looked at myself kneeling there with my head on my hands and thought 'Goodness, I must be dead, that's the only reason I'm up here,' and at that point I zoomed back into my body. For a good few years, five or six or even seven, I didn't understand what had happened but then a friend of mine gave me a book on the occult. On reading the section on astral projection I realized that this was what happened to me that day in the church.

How can you go astral travelling? Visualization is all important so learn to visualize really, really well. Start with simple objects in the room around you. Shut your eyes and see them in your mind's eye. Go on to more complex and detailed objects such as paintings or a vase of flowers and then progress to seeing people and places. The most important thing is to sit quietly, relax and practise your own inner vision. Do it every day and then start to consciously project a thought such as 'I will visit such and such a place,' or 'I will go and see my friend who is ill.' The intensity of the thought will actually propel you there, given time and patience. Concentrating too hard won't help so don't strain or get tense in any way. Like most things, astral projection is a matter of practice and, above all, not trying too hard, too fast.

Astral Regions

The astral regions are where thoughts become real and where imagination can create or destroy whatever you please. This region is made of thoughts and feelings which have built up over thousands of years and have formed into a cloak in the air. The vessel that we use when we travel through this world of thought is called the astral body. In shape it is like a faint image of your physical body and, although it is transparent, everything appears and feels solid and very real. It can move just by thinking, so space and time do not have any effect on the body. The astral body is fixed to the physical body by a thin silver cord which can stretch as far as you can think. This cord allows the astral body to leave the physical shell during sleep or meditation without any danger. When the death of the physical body occurs the cord is separated and simply shrivels up. Sometimes, when you are woken up quickly and feel slightly dizzy or out of sorts, it means the astral body is out of alignment. Lying down for a while or going to sleep again will soon bring it back into place.

The astral regions are not like layers of jam in a chocolate cake, but more like different coloured bands in a rainbow where one layer mixes into another. The astral regions are composed of seven divisions of which the first three are not very nice at all, because all the mischievous forms and clinging beings live there. These regions have been created by all the clinging and selfish thoughts and feelings we have had over thousands of years. Gradually, enough clinging and selfish thoughts come together and take a form of their own, and its driving force is the clinging and selfish energy behind all those thoughts and feelings that have come from our human minds. The forms these thoughts grow into are similar to the horrid-looking creatures you often see in books about the underworld. These cannot really hurt you at all and rely on your fear of them to feed their forms. Luckily, most people travel past these regions without any problem and it is only if you have any nasty traits that make up these regions, that you are drawn towards them.

The next four layers are much more pleasant because the thoughts and feelings that have created them are much nicer. The fourth region is the resting place for the people who have physically died. They stay here in a state of slumber while they are preparing to move on to the next part of their journey to the spirit planes. The fifth region is that of the intellectual and artistic activity connected with the earth; many musicians and artists tap this region for their inspiration. The next region is where all the heroes play out their victories that they have had on earth and, although heroism is a fine act, some people get carried away with it and therefore they have to repeat their heroism again and again until they understand what it is really all about.

The seventh region is that of the mystics and great religious minds from earth looking after and teaching mystical and religious knowledge. In Christian terms it would be seen as heaven, or to a Buddhist it would represent Nirvana.

Beyond these regions lie all the mental and spiritual realms which cannot be reached unless the individual is in harmony with their vibration. It is the vibration inside you that counts. If you only care about your needs you will not be able to enter into the vibration that is caring and unselfish, not because someone has judged this to be so but because you would not feel happy being exposed to that type of vibration. If you are ever exposed to truth and love, before you understand and accept it, you will find that it will make you feel extremely uncomfortable because it will immediately start to move everything inside you that is not truth and love. If that happens to 60 per cent or 70 per cent of you it will feel like your stomach is dropping through your feet!

It is quite natural for everyone to travel around the astral regions during their sleep, and many people do this consciously and remember what has happened. An occultist or magician uses the astral regions to do work because spells, curses and magical rites may go through a physical act but it is in the astral regions that they have the most effect. For most of us, though, the astral regions are places where we can sort out things during sleep, or meet people we are in dispute with to find a solution, or perhaps to get inspiration or help from one of the teachers in spirit.

Astral regions are the middle ground between matter and spirit and the mixing and mingling between the two is a very natural part of our existence.

You can direct your astral journey at night by asking yourself if you can see somebody or talk to somebody you are in conflict with. Or even just say to yourself that you want to see something beautiful or meet your guides. You may not remember consciously what happened in your journeys but they will be part of you and gradually, as you develop, you can travel consciously around the astral regions and become aware of what is happening. If you do try astral projection, that is, travelling into the astral planes while you're in a fully conscious state, just be sensible and, if you get a fright, do give it up until you meet someone who can help you to do it properly.

Aura

Everyone has an aura and so does every plant and animal. The aura is an electromagnetic field of psychic energy which varies enormously in width, depending on the spiritual state of the person. Halos around some of the masters and saints, as depicted in paintings, are the aura, although they are usually painted around the head and not the rest of the body. Can you feel the aura? Yes, indeed you can, and very easily too. If you place the palms of your hands together, then slowly pull them apart until you feel a slight tingling you'll know the width of your aura. You can even feel, as you repeat this very slowly, the energy build up between the palms of the hands and you can, in fact, bounce the energy from one hand to another. By simply joining the hands together and pulling them apart, the tension grows.

You can learn to see the aura through training and, at the beginning, it appears as a light or shadow around the body. As your training progresses, you are able to see bands of colour in the aura. Colours show not only the health of the person but the emotional state as well. You can always tell a liar by his aura. A healer often sees a shadowy patch near the afflicted part of the body, and is able to diagnose suitable treatment as a result of this. As you grow in spiritual knowledge, then your aura can enlarge. One way to help you do this is to bathe a great deal in sea salt or in the sea. Sea salt actually increases the electromagnetic field and I find that if I have one or two sea-salt baths a week, I am much clearer and brighter psychicly. Do remember, however, that sea salt dries up the skin and you don't want to end up looking like a prune, so twice a week is fine to start with. Certainly, taking salt baths makes everything sparkle and brightens psychic ability.

When you can see auras, you'll be able to detect those who take energy from others, simply because they don't have an aura themselves but have, instead, a black line around the edge of the physical body. Rather like a black hole they absorb energy when they need it, as they seem unable to store it for themselves. I am sure you have had the experience when you have been ill or short of energy, and various people have come to visit you, that after some of them have been to visit you you'll feel distinctly better. But others, however much you love them, make you feel drained and exhausted. I don't really like the name vampire, but that is what these people are, and most of them would be quite shocked to realize it. It is fine when you have the energy to give, but you need to seal up the aura through visualization when you are near people who have this affect on you or, better still, see less of them.

A confused and anxious person would have mostly a grey, cloudy aura while a particularly spiritual and uplifted soul tends to have a blue or indigo one. The aura changes all the time and is a fascinating kaleidoscope of colours as well as information. You can even buy aura spectacles to help you to see the aura more clearly. These alter the retina of the eye enabling it to respond to rays of light which are beyond the visible coloured spectrum.

Automatic Writing and Psychic Drawing

Many people do automatic writing and regard it as quite a normal phenomenon, which indeed it is. Simply sitting down and holding a pencil or pen lightly in the hand over a sheet of paper and waiting for it to move is all that is required. Thinking of something entirely unconnected with wanting your hand to write is also a help. Your hand could eventually begin to move and marks are made on the paper which may or may not develop into writing. This writing is produced without the conscious participation of the writer and there are plenty of examples of someone in spirit communicating through a medium in this way. Not only is the writing the same as when the communicator was on this earth but even the style and character are sometimes identical. The writer's self-conscious mind could, however, influence the result and needs to be looked at.

Automatic writing, like automatic art, is, by its very nature, not consciously produced. The English mystic, poet and artist, William Blake, depended upon mystical visions to inspire him. Not only did he claim that most of his poetry was dictated directly to him by dead poets but also that his engravings or watercolour paintings were either sparked off by unusual visions or helped along by unseen hands. He also stated that the secret of etched copperplate writing, which he perfected, was revealed to him by the spirit of his dead brother, Robert, who, before he died, was an aspiring artist.

The person who can produce such works is often called an automist. Some automists are completely unaware of their surroundings and their actions and they are often surprised to see the work they have put on canvas or produced on paper. Other people who work in this way become drowsy when they work and are only vaguely aware of their hands and what is going on through the motions they are making, whether it is drawing, painting or writing. Others are totally conscious of their allowing someone to use their hands and create something under guidance. An automist who produces automatic writing often develops a unique style and shows fluency of expression. If you feel you would like to do this, you will probably start off with a hotch potch of doodles and marks on the paper but do persevere if you feel strongly motivated. Everything requires practice and this above all.

I have met two psychic artists and one has become a dear friend. I find that it is tremendously useful to have portraits of those who help me and who are part of my spiritual family. It is wonderful to feel the energy and personality through a portrait but also it helps a great many other people who come to see me, who will have known the people I have on my walls. I never tell my visitors who they are but they often tell me! It is enough to trigger the memory in their minds by simply having the portraits available to them. A psychic artist is very much like someone who does automatic writing, for the guide that is close to them will help them to draw or paint the picture that is required. My friend Coral Polge has a guide, Maurice De La Tour, who was a pastel artist in France in the eighteenth century. Coral's pastel portraits are by far the best she does. I have seen her reach in a box of chalks of perhaps a hundred or so, and, by simply letting her fingers move among them, to pick up exactly the right shade even though she has not glanced in the direction of the box.

If you sit with a psychic artist you may not get anyone you know, but certainly you'll find that someone close to you will know the people that have come through; often you will not get the person you think you wanted. Before I met my husband I had about eight drawings but I did not recognize any of them. When I showed them to him he knew them all, for they were all for him. This was years before we had even met.

Baptism

Baptism is the ritual of splashing or immersing somebody in water and was a natural part of life in Egyptian, Greek and Babylonian times. The Christian Church integrated this pagan practice into its teachings and nowadays the act of baptism represents membership and entry into a Christian community. It was thought that, if a baby died before baptism took place, it would be condemned to a kind of hell and also that the devil remained inside a child that did not cry during the ceremony. The use of water in initiation rites is based on the fact that nothing can live without water, therefore it represents the provider of life, clarity and the liquid of regeneration. By using the purest physical element, such as water, it was hoped that the regeneration would come about by invoking the spirit of life to enter the external and internal parts of the body. By doing this the door within would be opened so that the spirit of truth and clarity would enter the life and become a guiding force for the individual and family.

It was already a fundamental part of religious activity to baptize people, but the baptism of Jesus by John went further and included the Creator in this act of regeneration. What it meant was that the unity between fire and water, the heaven and earth, was being united. This was symbolized by the Star of David. It was an opening of the door to other doors of energy so that mankind would be exposed to a new force, that of the Cosmic Christ, which is not a person but a vibration. Water also took on a greater importance because it represented the beginning of the Piscean Age, the age in which the element of water had the biggest influence and the age in which a period of cleansing and purifying had to happen before the next stage. Remember that John the Baptist said that he baptized with water yet one would come who would baptize with the Holy Spirit. This second act of baptism comes about when you have overcome the physical limitations and reached the point of changing from the physical being to a spiritual being. This time fire or the Holy Spirit is used because it represents extension and purification at the highest level. This type of baptism or regeneration can only take place when you feel that there is no more fear, anger or selfishness left within you. It is truly the point when you can call yourself a human being.

Birth

The whole journey of birth starts far away in the spiritual plane. When you decide it is time to come back to earth, you first have to decide what you need to learn this time, and what will be the best conditions to bring this about. These things are discussed at length with your guides and helpers, and with your prospective parents. When this is all worked out you start to travel towards the earth, and on your way through the patterns of time you take on the astrological influences that you need to help you throughout your life on earth. You don't have a physical body yet but you do have a see-through body and you are able to travel by thought, so you don't get exhausted dashing across the solar system. So, gradually, you come to the edge of the physical world, the waiting room where many have come in preparation for their birth. You will be with your guides and helpers and maybe other souls that will be born at the same time. Here, you may meet old friends and make new ones, and generally it's a nice place to be. From earth, you get plenty of visitors who come to you in your sleep and you sort out the last-minute details with your parents. When the timing is right you will move towards the entry paths, which resemble giant helter-skelters, and, at the right moment, you literally jump into life, or sometimes you might need a little push. Gradually, though, there is a sense of movement which gets faster and faster; during this time you lose all full memory of the spirit world. The next thing that you'll be conscious of is the feeling of being extremely confined, warm, and in a semi-conscious state.

This journey can happen at the moment of conception or when the soul gradually enters into the growing child in the womb. Either way, when a birth is about to take place, there is much excitement and expectation and birth truly is a miracle:

Our birth is but a sleep and a forgetting:
The soul that rises with us, our life's star,
Hath had elsewhere its setting.
And cometh from afar.
Not in entire forgetfulness,
And not in utter nakedness,
But trailing clouds of glory do we come
From God, who is our home.

William Wordsworth
'Intimations of Immortality'

Black Magic

Black magic is manipulative and therefore against spiritual law. A black magician, however labelled, seeks to bend the will of others and impose his will with or without their knowledge. No human being has this right! Anyone dabbling in magic is incurring karmic retribution and should be well aware of the dangers they run. If you manipulate someone for whatever reason, and however pure your motivations or however evil, they in turn will, in time, be in a position to manipulate you. Think about it! It's interesting also that black magic doesn't seem to be able to exist without the use of ritual, yet the great masters such as Jesus Christ and the Buddha needed only the power of love. If the power of love can move mountains and the great masters of the great religions stood alone then why is it necessary to use ritual and power of the group to make black magic effective? Without his swords and wands and incantations the magician has very little left.

Does magic really work? Magic can be effective and powerful as is shown by voodoo in different parts of the world. But is it the *belief* that the curses and spells directed by a voodoo priest will work that makes them effective? There is no doubt that a voodoo curse can kill but there is a great deal of doubt that it can kill if you do not *believe* in it. Any act which is given energy will have far more effect than an act which is dismissed by the mind as mumbo-jumbo.

The aborigines in Australia can actually sing a man's death or use a pointing stick; by using their minds they can destroy their victims. Some African witch doctors have this power as well. Black magic is more intriguing than the gentler, less spectacular religion of witchcraft.

The black mass deliberately reverses the spiritual purpose and the symbolism of a religious ceremony. It's a form of ceremonial magic and the participants prefer to use a church that is used regularly for worship. Everything is desecrated, the crucifix turned upside down, the prayers recited backwards, garbled and foul substances burnt instead of incense. The sex act is often committed on the altar and even ritual murder is not beyond the people who practise black magic.

Any book giving information about rituals or the practice of magic was called a black book or book of shadows.

Breath

Your very first act in life is your first breath and your last act will be your last breath. The control of breathing represents the control of life, and it has been identified with the soul of man. In Roman times a close relative inhaled the last breath of a kinsman for it was thought that the soul needed to re-enter another body otherwise it would be lost. In Hinduism the breath or life current is seen as the force that controls the mind and that is why yoga always teaches breathing exercises.

It is very beneficial for everyone to do breathing exercises of some description because good breathing patterns and an increase of oxygen to the brain will make you feel good, mentally and physically. Some breathing exercises, which should only be done under supervision, will help you enter into different states of consciousness. These can become very strenuous for the beginner and can sometimes make you giddy, but they are very powerful and can invoke visions and dreams that are very clear. For most people, though, it will be good to make sure that you take a couple of deep breaths in and out, at least once a day, for healthy breathing is healthy thinking, is healthy being.

Burial Rites

The act of burial in carefully selected sites, with specially prepared stones and implements, suggests that primitive man did not see death as the end, but as a journey to another place of life. The idea of a journey after physical death is evident in every culture and every age. It has always been considered a necessary duty of the living to set the dead on their path to the other world, and the burial ritual has developed from this belief. In primitive times, symbols were carved on rocks and implements and weapons were buried with the dead to protect and help the passing spirit on its journey while, later still, when the idea of judgement developed, it became necessary to be buried with gifts for the gods so that they would be pleased and not consign the dead to hell. In Greece, a gold coin was buried with the corpse to pay the ferryman to take the soul across the River of Death. Yet it was the Egyptians who had the most elaborate burial ritual that lasted for days, for they believed that to secure your life after death you had to build a perfect duplicate of life on earth. The idea of a journey still exists today and flowers have replaced many of the earlier symbols; flowers providing the beauty, peace and tranquillity which it is hoped will help the spirit find such things in the other world.

The other side of burial rites involves making sure that the spirit keeps to the other side of death and does not return to haunt anyone. This was an important part of ancient ceremonies, and pagan and religious priests encouraged this so that people relied on their services. The important fact was that the burial ritual had to make sure that the spirit went on its way but, if the person was important enough, a contact with the spirit was hoped to be maintained. Many artefacts of the deceased were kept so that communication could take place by the witch doctor or the occultist, and these ancestoral spirits still play an important role in many places in the world. The burial place and the ritual involved create a doorway from this world to the next and provide a communication channel.

Gradually, burial rites in the West have taken on the idea of paying homage to the person and showing respect to the family. The ritual is a way for the bereaved to say goodbye to the departed spirit and to allow everyone to express their feelings. It is an important time because the bereaved need to let go the spirit so that it can go on its way, and the spirit needs to let go of its hold on physical life. The burial or cremation ceremony, therefore, represents a bridge between physical life and spiritual life.

Cartomancy

Our modern playing cards are often used to tell fortunes, but this isn't just fun or a party trick as more and more people are understanding, for our modern-day cards can be read in very much the same way as the Tarot. Said to be derived from the Tarot deck, there is indeed a close similarity between them. The swords of the Tarot are clubs, the pentacles are now diamonds, the cups are hearts and the wands are now called spades.

When you have a reading you will be asked to shuffle the pack, cut it and then to make a wish or ask a question as the cards are dealt out. Each card has a meaning and their positions on the table influence their significance. Having laid out the cards it is up to the card reader to use clairvoyance and ESP ability to answer your question. Sometimes you will be asked to re-shuffle and cut again as other questions come up.

A modern pack of cards of fifty-two consists of four sets of ten cards numbered from the ace or one up to ten, together with a King, Queen and Jack. There are four suites – hearts, spades, diamonds and clubs. Common methods of laying out cards are the star formation, the wheel of fortune, the quick seven, or the thirteen using the Joker. Most people who tell fortunes by cards are also using clairvoyance even though the cards themselves have quite precise meanings. There is an overall pattern for each of the suites and they are usually interpreted as follows: the dominance of hearts shows pleasure and happy marriages. The message is sensitivity (both sorrow and joy), but also warm and strong emotions and realized ambition. Spades are the cards of admonition and warn of danger ahead with possible ill luck. Diamonds are more concerned with everyday matters, particularly finances, law suits and the ability to work hard. They also concern stable family life as well as political success and profit. Clubs are the cards of loyal and worthy friends but can also mean treachery and disappointment, depending how they are placed.

Ceremonial Magic

This is ritual magic in which certain forms are practised by a group in order to accomplish a particular purpose. Ceremonial magic requires all the group to attend and the rituals can be quite complex. There is a strong interest in this type of magic in recent times and there are plenty of amateurs forming covens and working with the ancient practices. Magic can often prove very frightening and disturbing and serious distress can result from not understanding events. Psychological and psychic dangers cannot be overemphasized. Of all the areas of magic it is probably ceremonial magic that most approaches religion for those that are taking part. Some even regard it as this.

Chakras

These are power centres or energy centres in every human being. Pictures of the Buddha usually depict the chakra centres and these are seen as wheels or discs, seven in all, positioned in a straight line up the trunk of the body to the crown of the head. They can be perceived by the sensitive as multi-coloured discs that turn, each with their own rhythm. Starting from the lowest, the sex centre is the root chakra. The second is the sacral chakra situated in the area near the spleen, the third is the solar plexus situated at the navel, the fourth is the heart, the fifth the throat, the sixth is the third eye which is situated mid-point between the eyebrows and the seventh is the crown or the top of the head.

In any complex mechanism there are a series of centres. These centres control and relay information to different areas. They function from a central force but they have their own independency and their own ability to function at their own particular level. The chakras, the seven centres within yourself, function in the same way. They are centres that are independent, and they represent the seven aspects of a person. The seven aspects start from the base of the spine with the earthly parts of the person; the base where energy is drawn in and pushed out which is of a sexual nature, for the sexual nature is the receptive part of the earth. The movement is up from the earth, rising into the mental and eventually into the spiritual levels.

The seven points within you are the seven colours. Each has its own hue but they are capable of blending and becoming one. Different points need different colours for the chakras to function properly; where a point needs red it is useless to put purple, for it would only dislocate matters and make a very messy colour. When you are out and about, you have to do different things; sometimes you have to use your mind a great deal and so, therefore, it is the chakras and the centres that respond to the mental energy. When you have to respond emotionally, it is the green and yellow waves that are used and these are the ones that are working. The sexual energy is the energy at the base of the spine; while this can be used in a physical way it can also be brought to a

higher level so that base energy can be united and the spiritual and physical meet together. This is when the colours are able to merge together. The purpose of the chakras is for the spiritual and physical to come together.

Chakras are associated with various colours, although they are often a soft blending of the tone of the colour rather than a strong pronounced one. The colours I see are scarlet for the root, orange for the sacral, gold for the solar plexus, green for the heart, pale blue for the throat, indigo for the third eye and brilliant white for the crown. Not everyone agrees on these colours, but these are the ones I see and work with. The chakra centres continually turn – the meaning of the word is 'wheel' in Sanskrit; this is because energy is transferred from one to another.

If you find yourself out of balance or lacking energy in some particular point this is often caused by a blockage of a chakra centre. It is quite possible to use a pendulum to find out where the imbalance lies or, if you wish to deal with the problem without this device, then simply sense where you feel bad. Your life force comes through the crown at the head, so it turns each chakra as it reaches it, but if there is a blockage, for instance in the throat area, then not enough energy will get into the heart and the other chakras in the line. A lot of people have trouble with the throat area which is what we would call the trust area in emotional terms. This is also the cause of sore throats, colds and stiff necks! Perhaps you want to say something to someone that you can't or have said too much and regret it, or simply feel that you can't reach out to anyone at all. Whatever the reason the throat constricts and goes dry and problems with the physical body arise. Taking the throat as an example, you can reinforce the energy there by visualizing a pale blue colour turning the wheel, or, alternatively, wear a pale blue scarf or sweater.

Chakras not only apply to people but also to the earth itself. It is often said that there are several power points in Britain that help to give the British their bulldog characteristic.

In the West, earth chakras have been ignored until quite recently. The Chinese can show us how to understand the principle in respect of people and the universe, the microcosm and the macrocosm. Glastonbury is the heart chakra of Britain, its centre being the Tor, the pyramid-shaped hill with the spiralling path and ruined church tower dedicated to the Archangel Michael.

Charms

A charm really means a song or a chant and comes from a Latin word. Today, though, it is usually something spoken in magical terms and can mean much the same as a spell or an incantation. It's often said that someone has a charmed life and this means a lucky or protected one. Many people wear charms which are, in fact, talismans or amulets which are said to have power to bring protection or to bring luck. Again, if the belief is there I'm sure it will work, for it's the power of the mind that actually does the work.

Most people think that four-leaf clovers are lucky. Tradition has it that a three-leaf clover symbolizes the Trinity, a four-leaf one brings success, fame and a lover, a five-leaf clover brings wealth and money, and the very rare six-leaf clover ensures good health.

Clairaudiance

Clairaudiance, or hearing clearly, is the ability to literally hear, by extra-sensory perception, what is being said by someone without a body. This is a revelation when you start to develop as a sensitive for it means that you can hold a conversation and get answers to your many questions. Often the clairaudiant ability can come first and clairvoyance come second, as in my own case. For several years I was able to communicate but could not always see. I have described how my dog helped me to see earlier.

Often the voice you hear can sound from inside your head but it is quite possible to hear it from the outside, even from across a room. I often speak out loud as it seems to give emphasis and form to what I want to say; on other occasions I can conduct a quite complex conversation with one or more of my guides inside my head. I have a friend who writes books with the help of this ability and who has also developed a form of automatic writing as the words are heard in his head. This is a wonderful ability to develop for a tremendous amount of information and knowledge comes through at a very high level. It is, of course, quite possible to pick up the voice of someone who is living but this is more by telepathy than by pure clairaudiance. I have always found that clairaudiance is essential whereas clairvoyance may come later, for it is difficult to hold a conversation with someone who is just standing there and whom you can't hear! Ideally, of course, both are operating at the same time and this is the mark of the truly operational sensitive.

Clairvoyance

This means, literally, clear seeing or clear sight and anyone can develop it. A sensitive is a highly developed clairvoyant who uses this natural faculty most of the time. It is possible to be clairvoyant without the full opening of the third eye, situated between the eyebrows, but the clairvoyant is not likely to be very accurate on most occasions. There are many different forms of clairvoyant and, if you go to one, they may well ask to hold something of yours to give a better contact; this is called psychometry. This physical contact is very important for certain clairvoyants and many palmists; by the physical contact of holding a hand, for example, the clairvoyant operates more effectively. This is not the case with all palmists, those who follow the lines and have learnt their meanings. Clairvoyance with the use of cards or a crystal ball are other types of aid which help the concentration, and indeed, anything on which images may be focused can be used. In the past, the black mirror was often employed although this is now out of date.

Be careful, if you approach a clairvoyant, that you don't already have the answers in your head, for many have the ability to pick up from you telepathically. The best way to try out a clairvoyant is to simply blank your mind and just see what comes up, otherwise you are simply giving the whole story by thinking about it. A true clairvoyant or a developed sensitive does not need crystal balls, cards or objects to hold but simply senses at a higher level. An adept, however, who will also be clairvoyant, will probably not foretell the future for you, for the great advantage of living is the spontaneity of experience and, if you are told certain things about your future, this spontaneity will be destroyed or you could even try to fit the events into your life.

If you are aspiring to be a clairvoyant then do take your study seriously, for the power of suggestion is very great and you can influence people's minds and emotions in a very direct and positive way. I personally never give clairvoyant advice about the future although I often see things which are helpful when training a sensitive. I have found that most clairvoyants of my experience who work at the fortune-telling level, are very mixed up in their own lives; if you are choosing one you should look and see how happy they are and how fulfilled. If you really don't feel that you can put your life in their hands then they are not the person for you. Clairvoyance is also used, of course, to see spirit guides and spirit forms of those who have died and this can be extremely valuable in proving life after death to those who are distressed and bereaved. Here the advantage of being clear seeing is one often of mercy as well as of love, for the death of a deeply loved one can be extremely traumatic if there is no strong religious belief to hold on to, and being able to connect two such souls can be a real joy.

Can you choose a clairvoyant for yourself? Unfortunately, the best ones never seem to advertise. You must, however, be truly comfortable with the clairvoyant and be prepared to trust him. A clairvoyant is as good as his spirituality is high. Think about it!

Many people join development circles at spiritualist churches or occult groups. It is up to you whether you wish to proceed alone or to join a group but do make sure you feel comfortable about it. Some groups give you the protection to develop your abilities but when that ability is established then the group 'mind' can limit the scope of your own clairvoyance. In other words, it is often good to start off in a group but you need to know from your inner voice when you need to leave. It may be better to develop on your own than to become influenced by the thoughts of others. A good development circle will probably start with ten or twenty minutes' meditation and then perhaps practise psychometry among the group, passing jewellery or personal objects such as a coin or even a key to see what can be got from its vibrations. There is a practical use of ESP. When you first start to develop you often get several aches and pains, particularly in the head and around the area of the third eye. Headaches are quite common and mean that something is happening, so welcome them. No doubt ESP can be enlarged and refined but it certainly cannot be conjured up and not everyone has the ability or capacity to freely demonstrate it. Choosing a group means choosing the teacher as the teacher will surround himself with sympathetic subjects. Seek an interview with the teacher first and listen very carefully to what he says and asks you. You can certainly blossom in a supportive and hopefully comfortable milieu, but if you are not being treated as an individual as well as a group member then the group probably has little value for you.

I am often asked if mind-control classes work. I have had several people come to me who have done these courses and who seem very confused indeed, but I really cannot judge from this. The answer is that, if the course is offering a certain success rate connected with your ESP ability, I would have doubts about its validity. This is simply something that cannot be promised or bought. You are an individual in your own right and you will develop in your own way and in your own time. Nothing must be forced or pushed or manipulated and, if it occurs, then, please extricate yourself from the group or the teacher and ask guidance to find someone else. The wonderful thing about working spiritually is that, when you need the teacher, the teacher always appears.

Collective Unconscious

The collective unconscious is a term first used by a psychologist called Karl Jung. His investigations into the human mind led him into mystical realms and he found that in every civilization throughout history, there were expressions of the universal forces. These common themes, or archetypes, were always in symbolic form and only came into the conscious levels of the mind during an altered state of consciousness, in dreams, meditation or through art. From this evidence he developed the theory that there was a common bond between all mankind, and that there was a point where the collective forces of Man's experience not only met but could be shared. It has never been established whether the collective unconscious is a common pool that we can all tap into, or whether each individual carries within himself the sum total of the collective unconscious of the whole.

Some examples of common themes or archetypes are the belief in the idea of God, the creation of the universe by God, and the divinity of mankind; the most well-known archetype must be the demon or Devil symbol. This has appeared in some form or another in every belief system around the world at every moment in history. The Devil is basically used as a scapegoat for anything that is undesirable or bad, but really the Devil is a mirror of what is inside ourselves. For Jung, the God image represents the archetype of the self; he came to the conclusion that wholeness whether in normal development or as a stage in the recovery of a mental illness, comes through finding the God within ourselves.

Communicating with Plants

Everyone feels better in a garden or in a forest and if you live in a city and feel out of sorts your first thought is to get away into the countryside to be in touch with nature.

So what is it about being close to nature that makes us feel so good? It is simply an exchange of energy between ourselves and the plant kingdom. Most of us have more vitality than we need for survival; particularly between the ages of eleven and thirty it is thought that we have as much as 75 per cent surplus energy. Plants also have surplus energy and it is quite possible to exchange energy with the plant kingdom. This isn't, however, done by the modern gardener who uses mechanical implements and petrol-driven appliances. The energy that is given into the air is simply burnt up by such things and nobody benefits. It is the old-fashioned gardeners who know all about composts and call manure, manure, that really come into their own. The ability to have green fingers is the ability to love and care and understand what is going on in the plant kingdom.

Human beings are the highest kingdom on earth and we are able to communicate and control all kingdoms that are beneath us. Therefore it is quite easy on a particular mental level and emotional level to communicate with plants, because they are living beings. They have their own particular life force that a human being can tune into so that there is a communication. It is not like speaking or even thinking, as it does not reach that level, but it does have a mental frequency and is probably more of an emotional nature; even that will not describe the communication in the right context, for the plant just *is*. Plant energies have special qualities. They have a special obligation to provide for other kingdoms above them and this they do in great abundance.

The Findhorn community in Scotland has demonstrated, by talking to the devas of the plants, that it is possible to receive a ceaseless flow of metaphysical truths, useful gardening tips and, as a result, a bumper harvest. In the early 1960s Peter Caddy, his wife Eileen and Dorothy McLean, who were both sensitives, were guided to live in the Findhorn Bay Caravan Park. Findhorn is a drab, windswept little town on the North

Sea coast of Scotland about thirty-five miles east of Loch Ness. In this unprepossessing site and chill northern climate, Peter Caddy was asked to plant a garden. A garden in the sandy, apparently infertile soil? Yes, and, what's more, by using mulch and natural fertilizers and seaweed he grew the most astounding vegetables in his first year. The locals marvelled and questioned. Gradually, the garden became national news and horticulturalists and experts flocked to see the prolific yields on sandy soil. Forty-lb cabbages were the norm.

How was it done? Peter says, 'Since it is love that fulfills all laws, it was my love for the garden that put me in tune with it.' Dorothy McLean, particularly, had long sessions talking to the devic forces and produced useful information about how to plant, when to plant and if to plant at all. As there is a deva for each type of plant, vegetable or fruit, she certainly had a busy time. But very, very rewarding.

There is no doubt that many people today talk to their plants. Some even have names for them and I do myself. Why not christen a plant today? Some people believe that prayer helps to increase the growth rate, and in the 1950s a minister in California found that, by prayer, he had a 20 per cent increase. Certainly music has a very strong effect on plant growth. Recent experiments have shown that the type of music played to plants affects their growth. Disjointed and inharmonious sounds, such as modern rock music, don't do a lot for them, but classical and harmonious tunes certainly do. So the choice really is between Bach and the Rolling Stones!

The ability to communicate well with plants must stem from love and love means caring. If a plant is ailing then simply sit down with it, close your eyes and allow the plant to communicate its needs to you. These aren't obvious needs necessarily, such as more water or less water or perhaps feeding, but it can be that the plant wants to be moved, to be near other plants, or indeed to go from outside to inside the house or vice versa. Is it happy or sad? Perhaps it needs repotting or perhaps it simply needs more care, attention and appreciation from you. This is not the plant talking to you, but rather the plant communicating with you on a very subtle level and you have to be extremely quiet and very still to allow the quiet vibration of a plant to communicate. I also find that planting a crystal into the soil near an ailing plant is a wonderful remedy so long as the crystal is programmed to energize the soil around the plant. This certainly is a booster that has no comparison. Try it and see.

Crossroads

Crossroads are uneasy and uncanny places for they offer a choice of routes which are symbolically seen as paths through life, with dangerous possibilities if the choice is wrong. The physical and mystical choice at a crossroads has always been significant and in olden times suicides were always burnt at crossroads because their ghosts were expected to be restless and vengeful. Usually a stake was driven through their heart to prevent them from moving. Criminals, whose ghosts were also expected to be vengeful, were often executed at crossroads to stop them from roaming about. In Russia, vampires were believed to lurk at crossroads ready to attack travellers; in Japan phallic symbols were placed at road junctions to protect travellers. In India, offerings were made to Rudra, the God who rules ghosts and evil powers. On the brighter side of things, American Indians buried their dead babies at crossroads thinking that their ghost would 'enter' passing women and so be reincarnated. Also in America, when you wanted to get married, the suitors were invited to meet at the local crossroads so that you could be sure you had the best choice. Perhaps this is not such a bad idea after all!

Crystal Ball

More often than not this is a polished ball of glass or, more rarely, crystal that is used as a focus for a medium to see the future. Seeing the future in this way is also called scrying or crystal gazing. The crystal ball is also known as the watch ball. Any psychic person can use a crystal ball as a focus but, as they become more involved, they are able to do without such things as crystal balls, packs of cards or even palm reading.

Curses

There are a great many curses that are produced every single day by a great many people. A curse is the intention of a thought that is formed quite strongly in the mind and then projected out. It surrounds whatever you are angry or upset about with a great deal of force and a great deal of restriction.

We tend to think that curses only existed in ancient times and it is true that, in those times, we were well versed in all of these arts and produced terrible curses. Much of the time these curses were only produced to protect the things that were respected and honoured. Anyone who disturbed these things, especially in the pyramids and the tombs, took the brunt of curses. If the trespassers had knowledge and respect they could have averted some of these curses.

One of the most famous Egyptian curses is connected with the tomb of Tutankhamen. He was a boy king who died before he was twenty. The entrance to his tomb was discovered in 1922 by an archaeologist named Howard Carter. Several curses were inscribed on the walls on the tomb entrance, warning of the calamities that would befall anyone disturbing the king's rest. The archaeological expedition was sponsored by Lord Carnarvon and, on the discovery of the tomb, he was cabled to meet the expedition before they entered inside. Carter completely ignored the warnings and both men entered the tomb together. Shortly after, Lord Carnarvon became ill as a result of an insect bite and died without regaining consciousness. That night, all the lights suddenly went out all over Cairo and Egyptian newspapers blamed the death on the tomb's curse. Lord Carnarvon's dog in England began to howl and then dropped dead at the same time as his master's death. Since 1922, more than twenty deaths have been connected with the curse of King Tutankhamen's tomb.

Another Egyptian curse caused a stir in 1881 when Douglas Murray, of the British Foreign Office in Egypt, purchased a mummy from the Egyptian government and brought it back to England on the same ship that he was travelling on. The ship had only been sailing for two days when he was found dead; he had apparently shot himself in the head. His assistant took over responsibility for the mummy on board but found that, within a short time, he had become completely bankrupt. He therefore felt that it would be best to be rid of the mummy and sold it to a London antiquarian who immediately presented it to the British Museum. The mummy was carried into the museum by two men, one of whom broke his leg and the other died suddenly the next day. Wallis Budge, the curator of the museum, had the mummy photographed as soon as it arrived, and was surprised when he discovered that the mummified figure was a woman. The photographer also died immediately after photographing the mummy. Dr Budge decided to have the wrappings removed and found the body of a well-preserved, female corpse and, deciphering the inscriptions on the mummy's case, it was found that she was a priestess of the God Anon-Ra of Thebes, whose priests and priestesses were well known for their magical powers. All these strange events were reported in the British press, and visitors to the museum were often scared by the sight of the mummy. Therefore, the British Museum decided to sell the mummy to an American who immediately had it shipped to the United States. The mummy never reached America for the vessel on which it was travelling, the SS *Titanic*, tragically sank on its first voyage.

For the everyday person, curses are of a much milder manner but are still extremely destructive. If all the curses produced in one day were put together, the force would be equivalent to one by an Egyptian high priestess. If you hate somebody or are angry and you cannot control that anger, you are literally cursing someone with your thoughts of anger or hate. This hate causes much destruction and, worse than that, it will also swing back onto you. So, when you are angry, do be very careful.

A real curse is the conscious effort by somebody to formulate a very powerful set of words or actions. A great many of these are known in the area of witchcraft or magic. The same forces are used but in a very conscious way, projecting towards a person or situation, usually for destructive or selfish purposes. Sometimes, people think there are curses on them but really it is only their own energy that is in conflict with themselves or the people around them. If that energy is not able to find somewhere to flow, it will cause destruction in surroundings and within the individual. This to you may appear as a curse, but in fact is your own curse.

If you believe in a curse it will probably work so the best idea is to disbelieve the other person's ability to curse you. Giving him credit for being able to curse and to put a spell on you is like opening the door of your house and letting in an assailant. Curses are auto-suggestive. You don't really need to be the willing victim and suffer the misery that can be caused by believing what is being said. Sealing your aura will help, so imagine yourself with a large egg around you, the shape of the aura, and simply seal it up, surrounding yourself with radiant white light.

She left the web, she left the loom,
She made three paces thro' the room,
She saw the water-lily bloom,
She saw the helmet and the plume,
She look'd down to Camelot,
Out flew the web and floated wide,
The mirror crack'd from side to side,
'The curse is come upon me,' cried
The Lady of Shalott.

Alfred Tennyson
'The Lady of Shalott'

Death

If we knew how marvellous death really was, we would pop off immediately! For with death there should be no fear. It is just the same as when you're asleep, except that you are always conscious of where you are going, and it is a perfectly natural process. Over the centuries many religions have had a great deal of power by making death a fearful thing; have extorted a great deal of money from people with promises of a better after life; yet none of this is true. You judge your own soul always, and although friends and helpers can advise you and comfort you, at the end of the day the answers always lie within you. Heaven and Hell are firmly on the earth, for you make your own heaven and your own hell in the way you live your life.

It is interesting that in the last few years several books have been written about the experiences of people who have technically 'died', then come back to tell their story. Mostly these are through accidents; the effects of anaesthetic after an operation or a heart attack. Without exception they all follow the same pattern. However much pain and discomfort the physical body has been suffering, the moment the soul gets into the astral body this disappears and there is a marvellous feeling of lightness and peace. Invariably, a loving soul appears to talk to the person, and if their time on the earth is not completed and their purpose not fulfilled then they are advised to go back. That marvellous feeling of peace and at oneness stays with them, however, and their lives frequently take a turn for the better. Death is a beautiful process just as giving birth is a beautiful process. It is simply the end of a cycle, for the soul goes on eternally learning lessons and seeking perfection. It is also worth mentioning that those who have gone before you are not necessarily separate from you at all. Often they choose to be close to you for as long as is necessary. Our whole attitude to death needs to change radically, and even though the Irish get very close to it as they rejoice with their wake, most religions see it as a dismal and sorrowful occasion. Yet it is a blessed release and the beginning of a new cycle for the soul that has gone on and is indeed a time for rejoicing. If you cry, wail and mourn, you are literally holding the soul to the earth and this is doing you and the soul no good at all. The truly loving person will know in their heart that release from the physical body means the soul is free to progress and will not attempt to hold it in this way. It is most distressing for the departed soul if loved ones continue to mourn. As more and more sensitives become trained this attitude must change, for at the funeral itself, the soul can be seen together with the ones who are already on the other side welcoming them. There is always a lightness and a joy attached to this meeting, and it is possible to share in it. Wearing bright colours and avoiding wearing black is all important too. Of course, for the one who is left behind there must be a feeling of loss and emptiness, but it is the truly loving person that transcends this and sees the truth.

Sooner or later you are going to find someone close to you will die, and you will have the experience of coping with this event. Most people when faced with feelings they cannot handle often repress them, so it is not so unusual to feel embarrassment about what to say to someone who has had a bereavement in the family, and indeed what to say to people who know you have had one. Gradually, this is becoming much easier, as death is no longer regarded as a taboo subject in society as we are more open with our feelings and thoughts in nearly every area of life. When my grandmother was dying I just knew I wanted to be with her and travelled quite a long way to spend three or four days to be by her side. We couldn't talk about death, but I thought it was a comfort for her to talk to me about her life. I remember sitting, holding her hand, looking out of the window over Glastonbury Abbey at the most beautiful sunset and her saying 'That's where I'm going.' At the church service I saw her presence quite clearly as did several others of my family, and she asked me to tell them that I had seen her and that she was all right. This was many years ago, but I did hesitantly do just that, although it took quite a lot of courage at the time. When my Aunt Kate died some years later I also felt I wanted to be with her at the end, and again made the trip to Somerset to be by her bedside. By this time I had been working as a sensitive for three years and had more courage to discuss death. We talked about it openly, and I felt my grandmother's presence very clearly and she, in fact, talked through me to my Aunt Kate. She kept saying to me that it was my total belief and faith in the hereafter that was so important and this, really was, in fact, what I had come to give her. Aunt Kate was a great practical joker, and enjoyed life in a huge way with great generosity and no pettiness. She didn't want anyone to mourn her and said so. The funeral procession had to go some way to the crematorium and there were about a dozen cars winding their way down a narrow country road. I think the joke really was Aunt Kate's for, at the first crossroads, a muck spreader joined the cavalcade. At the next turning a hay binder joined in, and as we were approaching the town a garbage truck! I could actually hear her laughing. Or did she plan it anyway?

I meet many people who have tremendous fear of dying and death and this fear has been perpetuated by religious belief. We actually die every single night of our lives when we go to sleep as the soul travels in the astral body. It is as simple as that and just as easy. I have done many hundreds and hundreds of recalls about past lives and the pattern is always the same. However the person has lived the death is always the best part. The soul simply floats above the physical body in total silence. There is much peace and such a wonderful feeling at this moment that I always allow the person I am working with to experience it for a minute or so. A gentle floating sensation, the end of physical pain and suffering and the ability to watch what is going on without any emotional response. I then ask them to turn away from their earthly body and look the other way and see who has come to greet them. The spirit guide is the first person they see, and the hand is outstretched and the kindly, loving eyes speak the welcome. Behind the spirit guide are friends and family and loved ones, all joyful and delighted to welcome you home. There is no fear; nothing is frightening. It will be the most beautiful experience of your life.

Death has always fascinated the living. Some cultures, such as the Egyptians and Christians of the Dark Ages have been absolutely obsessed by it. The Greeks and the Romans also have their myths and beliefs, but it has only been in recent years that death has been an acceptable subject to talk about and not a taboo. Religion is really the outgrowth of the fear of death and the dead, and most people pay homage to the church all their lives to make sure that their death will be peaceful and that they will go to heaven. What a shock they will have when they discover that heaven and hell are firmly on the earth!

Déjà Vu

The phenomenon of *déjà vu* (the feeling of 'having been there before', or 'having said that before', of 'having experienced this happening before') can either be a reincarnation memory or a this-lifetime memory, but certainly such things are always inherited memory. The senses trigger off inherited memory and you may find, for instance, that the scent of orange blossom, as it does for me, brings back the memory of a wonderfully happy wedding many lives ago, or that the smell of cucumber, which makes me instantly throw up, brings back a particularly painful and nauseating memory of the most extreme kind. The scent of roses gives me the most enormous pleasure and joy, and if I ever want to cheer myself up I go out and buy an armful of them! Memories of the past, undoubtedly.

Inherited memory of this lifetime is also important. I have a friend who lives in Portugal who is about to attempt to have a test-tube baby. She has done everything possible over the last fifteen years to have a child, and has spent considerable sums of money, time, effort and energy trying to conceive. I saw that she was blocking her own fallopian tube and so preventing conception. She was doing this through the power of her own mind and creating an energy block that was strong enough to do this. I then looked into her past in this life, to see what had happened. She is the second daughter and her mother had the most horrendous trouble with her first-born. Just imagine the terror and anxiety she must have felt when carrying her second child, my patient. All that fear had transmitted itself to the baby, so much so that the idea of having children herself, although on the surface one that was expected and socially accepted, was, underneath, a horrific nightmare. In coming to grips with this, she may now choose to release this block of energy and, with the knowledge that the fear is inherited, produce a perfectly normal child. Let us hope so for she is a wonderfully warm and caring human being.

Inherited memory is also a memory of the past. My dear friend Isobel has a strong memory of walking the spiral path around the Tor at Glastonbury. She has repeated this recently and during the two hours she spent circling the Tor seven times, round and round, many memories came flooding back. As a sensitive she was able to go into these with ease, but nothing would have then told her to walk straight up like all the tourists, which only takes twenty minutes. Some trigger inside her made her aware of the 'right' way. If you have the feeling as you go over a hill that you know exactly what is on the other side, even though you have never been there before, do pay some attention. Perhaps taking the time to stop your car or get off your bicycle and walk about, or simply sitting on the grass and allowing the memory to flood into you fully, would prove valuable and helpful. All too often we dismiss *déjà vu* as simply something that happens. Think how more interesting and exciting it would be to investigate it ourselves.

Demons and Devils

Demonology is a branch of magic that deals with spirits that wish to do ill to others. These spirits are considered to be supernatural beings that do not have divine status. The word 'demon' comes from the Greek term 'daimon' which means genius or spirits, and has been gradually distorted in the English language. A demon today is seen as an extremely evil entity. Demons are grouped under the four divisions of the four elements, although in some systems they are seen as shadows or ghosts. Gnostics, a heretical set of early Christianity, saw demons as direct descendants of the angelic hierarchy. Lucifer, or Satan, was supposed to have belonged to the most celebrated group called the Seraphim, before he fell out of favour.

Demons were supposed to have banded together and fought with the powers of good, and the great battle between good and evil lasted three seconds. Lucifer's forces were divided into four elemental categories: Zimimar was the King of the North; Gorson, the King of the South; Amayman, the King of the East; and Goap, King of the West. The whole force was said to contain 2400 legions, and each demon of rank commanded a certain number. Lucifer is not the great sovereign of this hierarchy. The real emperor is Beelzebub, Lucifer being the dethroned monarch.

As the hierarchy stands today, Moloch is the chief of the army, Adramelech is the Grand Chancellor, Astaroth is Grand Treasurer and Nergal is the Chief of Secret Police. Each country around the world is supposed to be under the protection of one of the demons. America is under the protection of Astaroth, Rimmon is in Russia, Mammon is in England and Belphegour is in France. The whole issue of demonology seems to reflect the duality of things, for each of the demons has a counterpart in the Angelic hierarchy. Demons represent negative forces and the angels represent the positive forces, but that is not to say that one is better than the other. There has to be a series of opposites so that we may be able to see between the two and know the truth of the matter. It is important to remember that demons can only have power over you if you allow them to do so. They can only exist if fed with fear, anger or hate. If these things are not in you, you will have no need of such forms.

Divinity

'So God created man in his own image, in the image of God created he him; male and female created he them.'

Genesis 1:27

Did this mean, then, that God was visually like a human being? If so, was he black, yellow, white or red? Is God male or female? The questions are numerous and can get us completely confused. God's image cannot be contained in a physical body, because he is everything; therefore, we must assume that the image of God refers to something that is not physical, something that is of the spirit. We must also assume that we were made with a part of this spirit, this divinity, within us, therefore part of God lives within us. We are clothed in a physical shell that houses our soul and our divine spark. No matter what our physical appearance is like, our inner self and our divine spark are the same as everyone else's, and cannot be crushed by physical forces. This means that we all have a drop of sunlight within our hearts.

For the person who denies any acceptance of the scriptures, we can turn to the simple fact that everything that exists is of divine origin. We all follow, and are part of, a divine order, otherwise there would be uncontrolled energies and chaos in our molecular structure; this is clearly not the case, there is a definite form of order. All the minerals, plants, animals, and humans follow an evolutionary path. In addition, mankind has a sense of purpose that is instinctive and helps him follow a highly developed path of evolution that takes him far beyond the natural evolutionary patterns. Our minds and intuition have discovered things beyond the physical world, and even our rational mind is discovering there are forces beyond the physical senses. These have only been found by a basic instinctive gut feeling, that scientists and sages have approached from entirely different directions.

Man, also, has an almost fanatical impetus to find out who and what he is, to find peace within his heart and mind, to find contentment and solve the mysteries that flow into him from outside and within himself. He wants to overcome and control his physical environment, his mental anguish and confusion and respond to the spiritual sense which usually manifests as religious or mystical investigation into life. So whether you follow the scriptures or look around you for man's history, there are constant references or examples of a powerful force that is part of our existence and the planet's existence.

This force can be called 'divinity'. One of the greatest tragedies of much of the human race is that we have hidden our divinity in such deep places within us that we find it difficult to believe that we have the ability and the power to raise ourselves beyond the limitations we place upon ourselves.

Nevertheless, we have part of the divine force in us, nobody can take it away no matter how restrictive our physical conditions are. The sage in the East has no more divinity than you, the only difference between the two of you is that he has bothered to look a bit further into himself and has seen that ray of sunshine within his heart. You can also find that ray of sunshine by looking much deeper, being less dogmatic, reducing your fear and believing in yourself. You have as much right to find your divinity, no matter whether you live in a council flat or own half the world. It does not matter what kind of physical, mental or emotional mess you are in, for your seed of divinity is the most powerful force you will ever come across and it is inside you, part of you, waiting to be released. All you have to do is to open your heart and ask for it to show itself.

Sometimes, when you have blocked your heart, you will get a pain deep inside – respond to that pain by feeling what the pain is saying to you. Do you only listen to your head or the cravings of the body? These things are necessary to keep your body together but over-indulgence stops you from becoming your real self. It stops you from tapping into your full potential. A newborn child has that quality of perfection and peace that beams throughout his whole body and spirit; we see it in him and yet, as he grows it gets buried deeper and deeper, as the physical world appears to be so harsh. But that does not mean it has to stay buried. Look at your fears, your pain and limitations, your loneliness, greed and inner violence and see that these barriers that you have built are all due to lack of understanding, lack of not being able to see what is true. They do not need to be there. By searching within yourself, and trying to clear away all the negative things that have happened to you, you immediately start to become clearer and stronger.

Dip into your own heart, really, really deep down and try to touch your own seed of divinity. Expose it to some light and fresh air, feed it with gentleness and kindness. Draw into yourself the sunlight and the beauty of nature, make a commitment to yourself that you wish to find that divine part of you that has been hidden for so long. If you decide deep down that this is what you want to do, you will find things will start to move at a profound level. Some of these movements may not be pleasant because you have to accept who and what you are and all you have done in your life, but isn't it better to start to live again inside, and feel something real?

You will also find that you start to draw people

towards you and are able to share your fears and worries with them. Knowing that others have had the same fears and worries as you will make you feel much more normal. You have to make the first move, though, and work really hard to get everything moving. It doesn't matter whether you have spent twenty or ninety years blocking all your divinity into a small box. You can still restart the process by deciding that you want to do so, even if you have no money or have no idea how to go about it.

Make the decision that you want to start living again and the process and the means will become available in whatever form your soul needs. Even if you get knocked down a thousand times by everyone around you, get up again, start to become strong inside yourself, not relying on exterior conditions to sustain you as much as before. Become real and take up your birthright and find your divinity within yourself, because it is waiting for you and has been from the moment that you were born:

'Wheresoe'r ye look, there is the face of God.'

Koran

Dowsing

Dowsing is becoming increasingly popular. Dowsing is the simple use of a pendulum, twig or rod to answer a question. A traditional dowsing rod is a forked stick, usually of hazel, which proved invaluable to our ancestors when trying to find water. By holding the forked stick and walking slowly, water was indicated when the stick bent or moved. It can actually twist so violently that it can break, and this method is still used in Mediterranean countries today. Peter, a friend of mine, has a villa in Italy and wanted to build a well close to the house. He asked the local priest, who lived some ten miles away on a nearby mountain, to come and dowse for the water which he then marked by placing a twig firmly in the ground. Unfortunately, some local hooligans pulled the twig up and the poor man had to come down from his mountain and repeat the process.

Dowsing may remain a mystery to twentieth-century science, but it seems that most people can do it, and it is certainly worth attempting as it is a fascinating hobby. The fact that dowsers, themselves, cannot explain exactly how it works doesn't matter a jot. If you are outside dowsing for water or minerals of some sort, then the forked stick can be replaced by a pair of rods or a plumbline which, according to tradition, should also be made of hazel wood, even though modern dowsers use almost anything, including metal coathangers! As you set off, you are supposed to concentrate, and even say out loud what you are looking for. Eventually, the rods will either cross, or the plumbine will swing, or the forked stick will suddenly bend down.

There are plenty of other ways to dowse that are far more comfortable than walking around the countryside, and, in fact, radionics is based upon the art of dowsing. I use the pendulum a great deal for medical work and healing. It is far easier to select one Bach flower remedy, the natural flower remedies, by using a pendulum, than to look at each of the thirty-eight remedies in turn. I keep the thirty-eight remedies in four boxes, and the pendulum lets me know which box I need, and then I choose the appropriate remedy. Try it. It saves so much time, energy and effort, and it even gets your patient interested in how to do it. Dowsing, medically, is a wonderful help to the healer as you can not only diagnose disease, but select the appropriate treatment. Usually this is concerned with alternative medicine, rather than orthodox medicine. I have a friend who is a very well-known homeopathic practitioner, who uses the pendulum to make every decision and every choice in his practice. When we started working together, I asked him to give up the pendulum for a whole week, and he eventually agreed to do this and to develop his intuition in a different way. I thought he agreed rather readily to my suggestion and found out later on that he had at home a homeopathic computer which he had just invented and had every intention of using in place of the pendulum! Luckily there is such a thing as divine justice, for the next morning when his first patient sat in front of him and his homeopathic computer was ready, he put his finger on the button and the thing blew up! Without the pendulum or computer, he was forced to use his intuition, and has done splendidly ever since.

Don't allow yourself to become obsessed with using dowsing methods. Remember they are a tool. After all, if you are in a situation requiring split-second decision-making, you won't have time to use the pendulum, hazel rod or metal coathanger. It is simply down to you.

Another way to dowse is to use the pendulum over a map to find almost anything. This works particularly well if you have lost something of sentimental value. Lost dogs or cats, even a lost lover, can be pinpointed quite easily and safely. There are many, varied uses of dowsing, and even the US Marine Corps are using dowsing as part of their training.

Metal-detecting is the sophisticated way of dowsing without using intuition.

Dreams and Dreaming

'All that we see or seem
Is but a dream within a dream.'
     Edgar Allan Poe
     'A Dream Within a Dream'

Dreaming is really an altered state of consciousness and goes on regularly each night as soon as we go to sleep. Statistics show that at least two hours out of every eight are spent dreaming, which is roughly a twelfth of your life. It also appears that the dreaming state and the non-dreaming state alternates. This can be seen by the restlessness of the sleeper.

Since the beginning of recorded history dreams have fascinated mankind, and the interpretation of dreams for the most part has been a complete riddle. It is true to say that we dream every night even though the dream may only last a few minutes, and there are many established dream laboratories now in operation that record sleep patterns and the effects of the body whilst dreaming. Rapid eye fluttering is an indication of a dream taking place and these can now be scientifically monitored. Experiments such as dropping water on someone's face whilst asleep and dreaming result in them having a so-called 'watery' dream about swimming or being in a storm. So many factors outside can also affect what we dream about.

Dreams can take various forms and the most common seem to be general impressions, hallucinations, realistic dreams and symbolic dreams. Many people receive realistic or symbolic dreams in connection with a future event, and if you are having dreams of a precognitive nature you need to take careful note of them. Usually such dreams occur very close in time and proximity to the actual event, and it is up to you to act upon them. It has also been discovered that dreams are often structured out of past events, but these events are rearranged into a future time. Symbolic dreams occur throughout the Bible, and the story of Joseph and the seven years of famine and the seven years of plenty is a good example. If you have dreams that occur in symbols then you must interpret for yourself what the symbols mean to you. For instance, if you receive a triangle shape in a dream it could mean something connected with a pyramid in ancient Egypt or it could mean the eternal triangle of a love affair! Only you know what it truly means. Most dreams tend to be impressions or hallucinations of some sort, but the impressionable dreams are important for many things that we hide in our subconscious can surface through the dream state without harming anybody. Most people dream of things they would not like anyone to know of, hidden desires or primitive urges that are safely released into a dream state and do no harm.

How do you remember dreams? Before you can interpret your dream you need to remember it, and there are several ways of doing this. Nothing is more frustrating than waking in the middle of the night having had a tremendous dream and then going to sleep again and completely forgetting it. The first thing to do is to keep a pad and pencil by your bed where you can pick it up quickly, whatever time of night you wake. If you are in the habit of waking during the night, during or after a dream, this is quite easy to do, so jot down every detail you can remember, however fragmentary, for often a dream will pick up again several nights later and the story will be elaborated on. Even if you have a nightmare do this, for if you never remember dreams, or it is such a seldom occurrence that dreaming is not a conscious part of living for you, then you can train yourself before you go to sleep. The most important thing is to train the subconscious and to remember, and this can only be done over a period of twenty-one days. It seems through scientific study that it is this period of time that imprints a desire firmly on the subconscious mind. Before you go to sleep become as relaxed as possible, physically and emotionally and repeat an affirmation such as, 'I will remember everything I dream tonight' or 'I will remember my dreams always'. You can make up whatever phrase you like as long as it is short, positive and to the point. Be sure to say 'I will' and not 'I wish to' or 'I hope to'. An affirmation has to confirm that the desire has already been accomplished or it has no power at all. Do remember that this has to be done for twenty-one days consecutively. It is no good missing a day here or there, otherwise it simply won't work. Give it a try – for remembering your dreams could change your life and be an insight into your past as well as your future. There are several books on dream interpretation which you can buy in any bookshop, but the best way is always to rely on yourself. No one knows your circumstances as well as you do and no one knows what symbols mean to you better than you do. So take all the interpretive books with a great big pinch of salt and always look to your own intuitive feeling about the dream first and foremost.

Often dreams can be confused with what is called, 'out-of-body-experience' or astral projections. Yet it is quite easy to distinguish between the two. In an out-of-body experience you are actually the centre of the action, whilst in a dream you are often observing what is going on.

Statistics show that over the last twenty-five years, of the dreams of hundreds of people that have been recorded, something like 27 per cent of them predict a future happening.

Often you have advance warning of what is going to happen which is called precognition, and dreaming the winner of the Derby or whether a newborn baby will be a boy or a girl is not uncommon. Warning dreams are also likely and can be of value in order to prevent accidents or rashness.

The most significant dream in my life is one in which all my teeth are pulled out. I am pleased to say that I still have all my teeth so this is a metaphorical happening, but each of the five times it has occurred, a major change has happened in life within days. Once someone I loved left me, and once I lost a child, and the other times I was going through major initiations.

Jenny says:

The dream I had was a true dream. I know it was, because when I woke up the next morning every detail of it was so clear in my mind and it had unnerved me, but it made me aware that in eighteen months my father would die. I was very close to my father and we had a very special bond, and I woke up in the middle of the night and woke my husband and told him this dream. I was back in my house in India in a flat with a balcony and there was a crowd of people on the balcony and we were watching a funeral, and I knew it was my father's funeral. I could see the hearse and I could see the coffin and I was quite upset knowing it was my father's funeral. Suddenly I felt a gentle touch on my shoulder, and I looked up and I saw my father standing beside me. I said to him, 'Dad, what are you doing here? This is your funeral, you shouldn't be standing here. The funeral is ready to start. We can't have a funeral without you.' Very gently he patted my shoulder and said: 'Not yet, my girl, not yet,' and I was getting very agitated. How could we have my father's funeral without my father in his coffin? I could remember that thought very clearly. I was getting very agitated and he stood beside me and once more patted my shoulder and said: 'Not yet, my girl, not yet,' and with that I woke up. As soon as I woke up the thought flashed into my mind: Eighteen months, that's all you've got him for. I never forgot that dream. My father used to come and have Sunday lunch with us every week for about three years before he died. After the dream, knowing that I would only have him for a further eighteen months, I tried to make every meal a special meal as if it were his last, and very often my mother would say to me 'Goodness how you spoil him.' But I kept the thought to myself as long as I've got him let me spoil him; I haven't got him for much longer, and sure enough within eighteen months my father was dead.

Sophia tells of her mother's precognitive dream:

This took place in approximately 1944 when my mother's half-brother Sebastian was the only Mexican who fought in the RAF. She had a dream one night where she saw him walking down a village all dressed up in uniform, waving and saying: 'They've got me. I've been shot. Tell Mother not to worry. You won't see me again.' And he walked down the village, through a lane and disappeared into a field. She woke up the next morning and she knew that her brother had been shot. She didn't tell her mother, she told her father. At that time her parents were divorced, and he said not to tell anybody, just wait and hear. Sure enough, about a month later they got a missing-presumed-dead telegram that he had been shot down over Holland. Well, after the war, because my uncle was a friend of Prince Bernhardt, he was found and buried in some special graveyard, and after the war, my grandmother and my mother went to Holland to Amsterdam to his grave. They had to drive out of Amsterdam into a village and when they arrived at this village Mummy saw the village she'd seen in her dream and she could tell the taxi driver exactly where to go. And she showed him: all the way down the road here; turn right here; left there. And they got to this field where she had seen her brother, and she walked straight up to the grave because she knew exactly where he'd been buried.

Dreams are a marvellous way of releasing excess emotion; whether it is fear, anger, hate, sadness or love, all these can be felt in the dream state. You can shout and scream, blasphemé or curse, and release these thoughts from your subconscious mind. Often dreams are not describable to others as they involve sexual perversions and the like, but this is the most valuable outlet that we have and a very harmless one.

Earth Shrines

Earth shrines, which were first thought to be burial and ceremonial centres, are to be found everywhere on earth. These include Stonehenge, the Great Pyramid and the Nazca Lines. The greatest concentration of earthworks are the 50,000 separate constructions found in a broad band stretching from Scandinavia to Italy. Some are dated to nearly 5000 BC and are so massive that they could not have been constructed in one generation. If you are sensitive to changes in energy, you will find that there is an increase in any energy activity at all these points.

Some places, like Stonehenge, feel like power stations,

and invariably these places are connected with other sites. The idea of placing stones in the ground could be a form of earth acupuncture where the energy of the earth is tapped into and re-directed. Recent studies have come up with the idea that many of the great stone rings were celestial observatories. This idea can be seen in the grid-like alignments, made up of 3000 stones, at Carnac in France, and the massive Indian medicine wheels of North America, but the most famous celestial observatory must be Stonehenge. We have to remember, though, that early man could not have dedicated much time and energy merely to understanding the stars. Early man may have had some intuitive understanding about the relationship between heaven and earth and used Stonehenge and other earth shrines for this purpose. All too often nowadays we completely miss these things because we are looking for rational reasons for their existence. There are so many earth shrines in every country, that were built over a vast range of time, that they form an important part of our history. If we understand what they were for, we will be able to understand more about ourselves and more about our planet.

The oldest Megalithic stone is a single standing stone in Europe dated at 4700 BC, while the oldest pyramid is estimated at 3000 BC. Stone circles were not constructed until around 2500 BC.

Stonehenge is one of the greatest of the ancient European stone circles and is situated on Salisbury Plain, being built by the Druids between 1800 BC and 1500 BC. It was used as a religious and astronomical temple and shows one of the remarkable achievements of pre-historic Europe, being made of massive stones carried 150 miles from Wales. The stone circle, topped by stone lintels, has a two-mile procession avenue and this was used to determine the midsummer sunrise, the summer solstice. Other stone circles such as Avebury can be visited and experienced today.

Ectoplasm

Certain mediums are called 'physical mediums' and ectoplasm is the substance which comes from them and can be used for the spirit body to shape. Ectoplasm usually appears as a slightly cloudy, fairly liquid substance, often from the head of the medium. Few mediums work like this today as it's no longer necessary to 'prove' that spirits exist. Earlier this century there were many fraudulent mediums producing large quantities of ectoplasm; in reality, yards and yards of muslin secreted on their person!

Elementals

The elementals and nature spirits are bodies of energy and are part of every living animal and plant and of the mineral kingdom. They support and help the life force of these kingdoms, for they look after all the things that are necessary for these kingdoms to grow and evolve. It may be strange for us to think that there are other forms that are not physical and need to look after things. Elementals feel quite at home in the form that they are in; they only know that every time that we are in contact with any of these kingdoms, we are affecting and involving that elemental. They, like us, are a body of energy that flows about and they do their particular work in the best way that they can.

Elementals are associated with the four elements of earth, air, fire and water. The earth spirits are gnomes, the air spirits sylphs, the fire spirits salamandars and the water spirits the undines. Elementals are also found as fauns (associated with animals) and dryads (associated with plants). Some are said to be mischievous, such as goblins and imps, but all are independent and exist side by side with us on planet earth.

ESP or Extra-Sensory Perception

There is no doubt that ESP can be developed and as we all have the potential for psychic experience it is not unreasonable that, by training, we can improve it. At the same time, although your ability can be enlarged it can't be conjured up, for not everyone has the capacity to freely demonstrate ESP. For instance, if you have a serious personality problem and tend to be neurotic you could find ESP extremely difficult.

One of the greatest assets in beginning ESP training is to be able to visualize. This is the ability to build up clear images in your mind and, if your normal way of thinking is not along visual lines, you'll have to train yourself in conscious visualization. One of the best ways is to find a picture (that appeals to you) which has a great deal of detail, and look at it with your eyes open, study it carefully, then shut your eyes and try to reproduce it in the 'mind's eye'. It is important to keep to as much detail as possible to stop your mind becoming bored! Many people suggest concentrating on geometric forms such as a square or triangle but this is not as effective at the beginning as a detailed picture. When you can reproduce a picture at will by shutting your eyes and 'seeing' it mentally then you can create colours as well. You don't have to do this at a certain time of day – you can do it on the tube or the bus, any time when you've got a few minutes of your own. You'll not only find this of great value to your ESP training but you'll find that your everyday living will improve as well as this training will increase your awareness of your surroundings. Building up clear visual images inside your head is of the greatest importance because only then can you project them outwardly and see them, for instance, on the surface of a crystal or a mirror.

If you wish to work with a crystal as a point of reference it must be real crystal, such as rock quartz, and not glass or crystal glass which has no psychic properties at all.

Having developed your creative ability and visual power the next best thing is to be able to still the mind. If you meditate already then this will be easy for you, but if you do not then you will need to learn how to meditate first.

Are you prepared to be an oracle? Many ESP subjects or clairvoyants have no need of the crystal ball or the tarot cards or any other device for centring the mind, for their gifts are highly developed and all they need is to 'tune' into the person or event concerned directly through the senses. Not only can these truly gifted souls see people in the spirit worlds but they can also contact beings in the elemental kingdoms, such as the devas, naiads and fairy folk.

Psychic or ESP ability has nothing to do with ethical or moral rules or with any particular cultural or religious outlook; it is a natural gift that is inborn just like character. Everyone has these faculties but with some people they are nearer the surface than others and with many they are so deep that it will take a long, long time to bring them into waking conciousness. The ability to see beyond the normal senses does not make us superior in any way but the range of our psychic powers does depend on our spiritual development. A great psychic can receive a great range of experience. The more lowly psychic can only receive what they can tune into.

Yet foretelling the future has its own pitfalls, for most ESP subjects or clairvoyants cannot steadily and consistently do this. A great deal depends on the relationship with their sitter for the mood of the sitter can influence the clairvoyant. We have all seen the fairground gypsy who reads tea leaves and coffee grounds but these are often used as a focus of attention rather than as a 'reading' of the shapes themselves. The power of the tarot cards, sand readings and, indeed, *I Ching* all lies with the ESP subject or clairvoyant, *not* in the tea leaves or cards, etc, or the positions taken up by falling I Ching sticks. The crystal ball is another example of an object on which the attention can be centred.

It should be remembered that, in the foretelling of the future, the clairvoyant enters into a close relationship with the inner lives of those who wish to know it. Anything that is said will have a powerful effect and be suggestive. Being a clairvoyant or ESP subject means carrying a degree of responsibility for you are entering someone else's world and stirring up their hopes and fears as well as their dreams. Being a good clairvoyant or ESP subject means not only unfolding your own power but learning how to control it. Only by being as accurate and as careful as possible will you be true to yourself. Highly ethical standards are necessary and working for gain should not be your goal.

Evil Eye

The evil eye is supposed to be a magical power some people possess. By simply looking at others they can transfer misfortune and ill-luck. Again, if you believe in

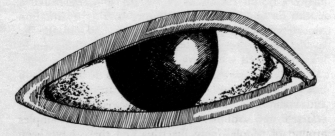

this it will work, if you don't it will not. Black magicians believe that they can not only acquire the evil eye through means of black magic but that it is also inborn in certain people. It is my belief that, unless there is fear in you already, you cannot attract such things and they certainly cannot harm you. Amulets and talismans were used and still are today, as protective devices. Having no fear is the only real answer.

Exorcism

Exorcism is a method of removing an entity or spirit from a body that belongs to someone else.

Through the centuries, priests have been able to exorcise demons and devils, often with bell, book and candle. Even today, if you feel someone you know is possessed, you can apply to most churches and ask for a priest to do an exorcism. Unfortunately, most priests today are neither developed psychics nor do they have any real knowledge of the astral planes. If you can't see what you're dealing with, it is very difficult indeed to know what to do. Now and then, of course, an outstanding churchman will also be a clairvoyant and everything works smoothly but, on the whole, praying and the sprinkling of holy water is not necessarily the answer. I understand it also takes something like a month for the person to be interviewed, the situation considered and a decision made to go ahead with the special service or not. By which time anything could have happened!

You don't have to be a churchman to do an exorcism but you do have to be someone who can fully see, hear and sense what is going on, otherwise you can get yourself into trouble. There are plenty of examples around of people doing just this and there have been many films in recent years showing how horrific the results can be. A possessed person not only affects himself but affects the whole environment, as was seen in the film, 'The Devils', 'The Amityville Horror' and also

'The Exorcist'. When these films were shown, the box-office receipts went sky high but so did the mass hysteria. It should never be forgotten that the film 'The Exorcist' was a true story which happened only a few years ago. A little knowledge is obviously a very dangerous thing.

So what happens in an exorcism? My first exorcism was someone who had come to me because of problems with her health which was deteriorating rapidly; most of her family were alcoholics. She was a young girl and a very beautiful one but she walked with her head held slightly on one side and had a particularly vague expression. When she walked in, I could see there were several entities attached to her head rather like Medusa, the mythological lady with snaky hair. The heads of the snake entities, however, were buried in her head, particularly on the side that she held slightly tilted. I was guided very carefully to find out from her exactly what had been going on in her life which caused this particular problem. Surrounded by so many alcoholics in her immediate family, she was constantly in an environment which was bombarded with entities attracted by their craving to drink.

Although she, herself, was not a drinker, it was enough that, when she was at a low ebb through an accident these things had attached themselves to her. I put my hands carefully into the aura around her head and willed the entities to depart in the name of the Christ force. What I had not been prepared for was the terrible squealing sound that accompanied this action; it sounded like pigs being herded into a corner. It was really loud and, although she heard nothing, I couldn't hear anything else. Gradually the squealing stopped and the entities were transmuted and all that was left was five holes in the aura. The second time I saw her, these had become scabs and eventually fell off as the healing was completed. This girl had no idea that this was an exorcism and I only told her that it was a healing technique after it was completed. For the first time in a very long time, she was able to balance her body. Not all exorcisms involve entities such as these. Others involve total possession of the person by another spirit and this can prove exceedingly traumatic.

A more common form of exorcism is to remove a ghost that is causing problems; you may also want to help the ghost on its way. My husband and I were holidaying on the Portmeirion estate in northern Wales, and were lent a smuggler's cottage off the beaten track. We had wanted a holiday by ourselves in order to get in touch with the earth energies and this seemed ideal; that is, until we opened the front door! A feeling of malevolence in the house was overpowering and I immediately lit a candle in each room. The contrast between the sunshine outside and this gloomy, heavy feeling inside the cottage was tremendous. We started upstairs and found three entities hovering about; two of them were husband and wife, previous owners of the cottage many years ago. They really were a negative pair and we helped them on their way very quickly indeed by simply commanding that they depart and ordering them out. The one downstairs was another matter for she was simply someone who enjoyed living there, having been the last tenant but one. Later, we found that her bones were buried under the floor. We gave her three days to make a decision about whether she wanted to go or whether she wanted us to move her on. The next three days, she spent walking behind me chattering about everything under the sun, including the way I cooked, etc, etc, etc. On the third day, she decided that she would like to go, and we created the energy space for her to do just this. At least this particular cottage will now be fine for families with children who must have, in the past, picked up these energies and had quite a shock, if not nightmares.

Don't rush in where angels fear to tread, however, and please, please remember that a little knowledge is not enough. Seek expert help every time.

Fairy Folk

Are fairies folklore or are they real? I have no doubt, from my own experience, that they are very real indeed as I have seen and talked to fairies. There is a great deal of interest today in the fairy people, ever since an article was published in 1920 by Sir Arthur Conan Doyle which included a photograph showing a little girl with fairies. Other photographs of fairies have also appeared from time to time, but I, myself, have seen several taken by, and with, Paul Solomon. Paul's photographs happened by chance. He was with a photographer when snow was on the ground and not very much scenery around, so there was no trick of the light, shadow or any other distraction. There is even one of him holding a measuring stick to measure the fairy by. The fairies I have seen, and Paul Solomon's fairies, are about six to eight inches high and are exactly as have been painted by artists throughout the centuries. The wings are like butterfly wings and they are perfect miniatures of the female form, very delicate, graceful and light in their movements. When you think of a fairy, you probably think of Shakespeare's Titania, the Queen of the Fairies, and Oberon, from 'Midsummer Night's Dream', or perhaps you think of Tinkerbell from Peter Pan. Everyone loves fairies as James Barrie found out by asking all the children to believe in the fairy Tinkerbell so that she didn't die, but lived.

When you were a child you probably read many fairy stories or had them read to you and the most marvellous things happened with these enchanting folk who could be fey or beguiling, as they wished. Fairyland is depicted as a timeless, hidden kingdom with a Fairy King and Queen and many winged, laughing creatures who sing and dance and occasionally get mixed up in the lives of humans. There are tales of changelings, of fairy children, of miracles and extraordinary happenings.

I often wonder how many fairy tales are based on a

semblance of truth, but here I'd like to stick to my own experiences. I've found at least two fairy circles in a wood in the Chiltern Hills in Buckinghamshire. I have experienced fairies dancing and, in one of the circles where trees had been cut down and then replanted, the forester had been sensitive enough to plant very small trees just outside the original circle. What a tuned-in person he must be! The time to visit these circles, if you are lucky enough to find one, is at dawn or the very end of an afternoon before the sun goes down. Sit nearby and wait and see what happens.

Can you see fairies? It is quite possible that you can but it all depends on your approach. Fairies exist in the realm of the sixth sense of man and simply cannot be seen with the usual five senses. If you want to learn to see fairies, then you must use the sixth sense, be very, very patient and learn to be still. If you go crashing through woodland talking loudly, disturbing the vibrations, nothing will happen, but if you go to the same spot at the same time each day, treading carefully and with sensitivity, and being extremely quiet, then you will be far more lucky. Simply lying in long grass and feeling the energies of the plants and trees will help you attune yourself to the environment. It is really the case of the fairy allowing you to see her and trusting you enough to come close.

My husband and I went to visit the fairy ring on the top of Whiteleaf Cross in the Chiltern Hills very early one morning, when the woods were empty. Empty? No. They were full of nature spirits, fairies, elves, gnomes, pixies and imps and we simply sat and waited. Gradually the whole forest started to move and vibrate. The leaves of the trees became silvery and almost transparent and, as our vision went into a different state of consciousness, it seemed that nothing solid was before us but everything was a sea of movement and shimmering light. It is then that we sensed the nature spirits and fairies. Nothing had been said and we hadn't moved. We had merely attuned ourselves to the environment and sent our love ahead of us.

Do try to do this for the experience is unforgettable, and is well worth the effort.

One of the things I have always wanted was fairies at the bottom of my garden but, as I live up in the sky in a flat with a roof terrace, I have created a corner especially for them. It's an area about six feet by four feet, and it is the most prolific and wonderful spot of the whole terrace. We don't go in there and water it from outside for it is their place and it is not for us to interfere. The fact that all the plants grow better and it is more overgrown and profuse than anywhere else, speaks for itself.

Do leave a corner of your garden wild and leave it for the fairies. All too often we forget these things as we control our immediate environment, lay out our gardens with beds and lawns and don't think of the other kingdoms who share the space with us. Perhaps you, too, will catch a glimpse of a gossamer wing or have a conversation with a gnome as I have.

Besides the enchanting fairy folk that work in our gardens and are found in the countryside, there are others who tend to love to dabble in human affairs, not always successfully. There are plenty of tales about leprechauns who cobble shoes at night or brownies who finish the household chores while the family sleeps, but also can hide that dustbin, broom or rolling pin if they feel like it. Dwarves are a type of fairy folk who mine deep in the earth for gold and precious metals and who make armour and jewellery. Even banshees are fairies who appear at the time of death to sing or howl (whichever way you like to put it) the dying to rest.

Banshee comes from Irish and Highland superstition and means fairy-woman. Banshees often appear as hags and usually attach themselves to a family or clan to become the family ghost. Their main function seems to involve a wailing and weeping session to let everyone know that a member of the family is about to die. In

Scotland she is often called 'The Washer by the Ford', because she is often seen to be washing the blood-stained garment of those who are about to die. She doesn't bring about death but is the witness of these tragic events. As you can imagine this is not the time when you would want to see a fairy.

Dwarves play a major role in nearly every folk legend and fairy tale. They are thought to be the little people of the world and range from the size of a man's thumb to the height of a three-year-old child. They are supposed to have originated either from the decaying flesh of the slain primeval giant, Ymir, or from the seas formed by the giant's blood. The gods gave them the wits and shape of man, and gave four of the dwarves, Austri, Vestri, Stori and Norori, the duty of holding the four corners of the sky. They also had magical skills and more wisdom than most mortals. It is believed that they lived deep inside the mountains, mines and underwater and their kingdoms and tribes are ruled over by kings who possess large armies.

Their main work was to look after old precious metals and jewels, and this guardianship included the glitter of the sun and the moon's rays. They are reputed to have vast stores filled with treasures and anyone who stole from them suffered great misfortunes. If somebody did steal something, it was thought to turn into a pile of dead leaves before it could be spent.

Dwarves are also renowned for their ability to produce magnificent metalwork, including armour for the gods, magic swords, rings and Thor's mighty battle hammer called Mjolnir, which always returned to the thrower's hand no matter how far it was thrown. Anyone who forced a dwarf to make any of these articles was doomed and brought misery and despair upon themselves.

The dwarves who lived in the mines were not such pleasant chaps and were blamed for broken tools, roof falls and sudden fires. This was only said to happen when the 'lords' of the mine had not paid their proper respect. If presents and food were supplied they helped the miners, giving them advance warnings of danger by tapping in the mine shafts. Their antics in and out of the mines were considered mischievous rather than dangerous, apart from the Black Dwarves which were a type of malignant elf.

Believing in the existence of dwarves has some rational justification for some of the first inhabitants in Western Europe were small, dark and shy people. They lived in dense forest that covered much of Britain, western France and Germany and were skilled in mining and metalwork. They lived quite happily until invaders from the East came. They were then forced to retreat to swamps and islands and were driven back by the clearing of forests for agriculture. It may be that dwarves are a memory of an extinct race with incredible powers and treasures, or maybe they still live in the deep forests away from the world of ordinary men.

You wish upon a fairy? Make sure it is the enchanting ones, not those who are tricksters and trouble makers!

Faith

It is easy to have faith in somebody who is true and full of love, yet how many people or ideas do we come across that are like this? To have faith demands a total trust and reliance on somebody or something.

Blind faith is sometimes necessary but, eventually, you should always try to have faith in your own truth and love so that you can find out who and what you are. When your faith is lost or broken, try to go back inside your heart to tune into your own love and faith. This will give you enough space to have faith in other people again, at a later date. Faith in somebody or something needs a lot of patience, because what eventually results may have gone through several transitional points, so don't give up before you have given your best and know that you have given enough time.

Remember, faith can move mountains. As the apostle Matthew said:

'If ye have faith as a grain of mustard seed, ye shall say unto this mountain, remove hence to yonder place; and it shall remove.'

Or Abraham Lincoln:

'Let us have faith that right makes might, and in that faith let us to the end dare to do our duty as we understand it.'

Fate

'Fatalism has its limits. We leave things to fate after exhausting all the remedies.'

Mahatma Gandhi

When you're born your book of life will only show the chapter headings and the page that gives you the birth experience. The rest of the book will be blank. How the book develops will be determined by how you go about your journey through life. It will depend on whether you take up opportunities and how you look at life and whether you deal with things or are overwhelmed by them. The chapter headings in your book determine the particular areas that you have to experience, but when and how you experience them depends on your attitudes and understanding. Development of the characters in the book, the adventures, love affairs and tragedies, will all evolve as you travel through the chapters of your life. Whether your book becomes a tale of woe or a great adventure depends on who and what you are. The forces of fate provide the frame for you to build upon, with whatever there is of your heart and mind.

At any time during your life you may decide that you do not want to write further in the book, and this choice is open to you. But remember that you will not be able to move on to the next page until you understand enough to write the final page. You may spend several lifetimes on the same page and, if this is the case, you will eventually want to turn over to the next page. Even if you commit suicide you will not be able to move on to the next page. All that will happen is that you will find it harder to reach the page where you left off last time round. When you do eventually arrive, you'll be faced with a very difficult situation and how you deal with it will determine whether you can move into a new chapter of your life. The length of each chapter is also decided by you, for some people understand something immediately whereas most of us need to make the mistakes fifty or a hundred times before we can see what is before us.

The forces of fate not only form the material for your life, but can also give you a little push. This can only occur when you have put your heart and soul into trying to achieve something and the desired result has not occurred. This push will bring about change and understanding so that you can become ready for the next chapter to be written. The end of the chapter may not have brought about the success that you thought was yours but the important thing may have been that you can let go of the desire to find success and allow yourself to move into the next chapter where success can be found without too much effort.

Your state and that of your family, your friends, your country and your world are all intermingled and reflect others as they affect you, but it is you that helps the quality, size and shape of your book through the efforts of your own heart and mind. Before you were born you consulted with your guide and helpers what would be best for the next stage of your development. You should remember that you are responsible for who and what you are and, if you look in the mirror and do not like what you see, it is up to you to bring about the necessary changes. Fate can sometimes direct you and sometimes help you to be in the right place at the right time. It is up to you to read the directions properly and decide whether you catch the right bus:

'Fate leads him who follows it and, drags him who resists.'

Plutarch
Life of Camillus

Fertility Magic

Fertility magic is probably the oldest form of magic and is connected to earliest tribal memories. The fertility of women was of the utmost importance. A barren woman was no good for the tribe. This kind of magic usually involved a dance imitating the animals that man hunted at that time. The male would then have sex with one or more females in the group. This sexual act was in order to stimulate the woman into conception. Witchcraft was often employed to make women have the ability to conceive, especially after several years of not doing so.

The maypole dance, seen in certain parts of Britain on the first of May, is part of the fertility magic carried through the centuries. The erect phallus is a symbol of fertility and those dancing around do so 'hopefully', in adoration and wonder! If you've ever danced round a maypole, or are about to, you know what you are supposed to be feeling!

Fetch

This is something nasty which is a projection of the black magicians's mind. It is usually a hideous animal such as a werewolf or even a vampire-looking human. It is merely a 'thought-form' but, as with all thought-forms, can take on a life of its own. The word 'fetish' also comes from 'fetch' as it is created by the mind of the magician.

Sometimes the magician, himself, gets into trouble when his fetch gets out of control and becomes more independent than he can handle. The only way for him to proceed then is to reabsorb the fetch into himself; this can be every bit as unpleasant as the experience that his victims have undergone.

Fortune Telling

I am not a fortune teller. Many people ask me to give a 'reading', but that is not what I am here for and I see very little value in it. Being a spiritual teacher, I am more concerned about showing people methods to enable them to know their purpose on the earth and discover a way to bring it about.

During my life, however, I have visited many fortune tellers, both as a journalist and as an investigator. Out of about twenty that I have interviewed nineteen were either using telepathy or simply picking up things from my appearance or what I said. Only one of them was genuine. The main problem with fortune tellers today is that clairvoyant ability does not come strongly all the time. If the reader is not having a good day, and their client has paid and is sitting in front of them, they have to say something and the temptation to invent it is evident. If you do frequent fortune tellers, make sure that you blank your mind before you go in, for it is all too easy for them to pick facts and names if you are consciously thinking hard about them. Most people have some idea of fortune telling, learnt from their grandmothers or from their neighbour next door. It may be cards, palmistry, tea leaves or a crystal ball. Often there is no harm in such activities but, to my mind, being told that you're going to have a crisis or that a crossroads is coming up for you in three months, can be of little use.

By our own free will we create our own future and can change our lives from day to day as, indeed, we can change the crossroads in three months' time. No one can foretell your decision until the very moment you make it and I often feel with people that, because a fortune teller has told them something they try to make it 'fit' into their lives, or simply worry themselves sick about the impending event. Usually fortune telling can do more harm than good in this way, and prevents our free creative spirits reaching ahead with confidence. Remembering that, in spiritual law, you draw everything to you that you need, even that accident that may lay you up for a month in order for you to think out which direction you're in, makes sense. I was recently hit on the head by a four-foot piece of plaster as a man fell through the ceiling and into my office. I was directly underneath and was propelled right across the room by the force of it. I remember lying on the trolley in the hospital saying, 'I don't have accidents' to an astonished doctor. My next thought was, why did I draw this to myself? The answer was that my family have a tendency towards curvature of the spine and the result of the blow has caused my spine to straighten which would never have happened to me otherwise.

Fortune telling has been practised since the dawn of history and, although many of the methods have changed, the purpose is always the same, that is, to gain hidden and mysterious knowledge and to predict the future. Through the centuries rulers have had their oracles and their seers and have asked about victories in battle and love.

So is there anything in it? Today, a clairvoyant, palmist or tarot reader will give you answers that you will understand. In the past they were often given in riddles or as omens. Fortune telling takes many, many diverse forms. In America, for instance, looking at an egg in water is still practised, animal intestines and charred bones are still used in Africa while other people use shells, tea leaves, coffee grounds and dice. Even candle wax and the way it melts can be used, notably in the

USA. *Fate* magazine of June 1973 says:

The client lights the candle and at the same time silently asks a question or makes a wish. Then the candle is tilted slightly, so that drops of the wax fall on to the surface of the water in the pan. The drops solidify into tiny spheres about 8th inch in diameter and float on the surface of the water. The first drops will go straight to the edge of the pan as if drawn by a magnet and gradually fill out a border. As you continue to drop wax drops begin to form symbols or patterns on the surface of the water. An inexperienced seer sometimes does not let enough wax fall. The more wax that falls, the more symbols are formed and the more complete the reading will be.

James Cole goes on to explain that, if the border is unbroken, this indicates a positive answer to the question, but a wavy border suggests doubt and a broken border only points to trouble. He also interprets a cat shape as an indication of trickery, a pistol suggests disaster or even death and an image of Venus points to love and peace while a jumping figure indicates change. So there you are!

Ghosts and Ghouls

'Hence, horrible shadow!
Unreal mockery hence!'

> William Shakespeare
> *Macbeth* III, iv

Everyone can feel an atmosphere and whether this atmosphere is comfortable, peaceful or joyful, or alternatively fearful and depressing, depends entirely on what has created it. An atmosphere of peace and love can radiate from the very stones of certain places which through the centuries have been true houses of prayer and praise. On the other hand other places create a fearful and malevolent feeling about them which can be totally negative. How does this happen? We are responsible for creating our own conditions, imbuing the place on earth that we inhabit with particular energy, and that energy will stay there for some considerable time.

Are there such things as ghosts? There is no doubt that ghosts exist! Throughout history there have been tales of ghosts and hauntings that are enough to make your hair stand on end. The tower of London is a wonderful example of this and is full of ghosts. Ghosts are souls who for one reason or another seem to be stuck and are still attached to the earth plane. Instead of finding their rightful place they have chosen to stay in the same place as they died. Often a ghost or wraith is a murder victim who had no warning of impending death, or is the victim of a trauma which is so great that he is unable to move away from it. Attachment to a particular house or environment through hate, greed, fear or other extreme emotions can result in a presence being felt there. Many suicide victims who haven't finished the work they set out to do in any particular incarnation are also stuck in the same way. So what happens if you sense a ghost or if one of your children can see a ghostly presence? The first thing to do is not to panic. The second thing is to turn and face the entity or try and sense where the entity is. Thirdly and finally, do communicate! Most people find this extremely easy once they have stood their ground, after all, if you can communicate and ask how you can help then there is more of a chance that the ghost will go once and for all. If you turn and run when you think you have come into contact with a ghost then it is most likely that *the ghost will run after you*! Put yourself in the ghost's position. If at long last you have found someone who could see or sense you, and with whom you could perhaps communicate, and then they turn and run away, obviously you would try to follow them. Most ghosts would reassure you that they wish you no harm, but not all! Often the ghostly visitation can change the temperature in a room, and most rooms with habitual ghosts tend to be much cooler and even more clammy than rooms that are not haunted. This is evident in certain churches. If you are faced with a malevolent ghost who creates a negative atmosphere then do seek professional help and ask for an exorcism. You need to find a sensitive who is used to this sort of work. Relying on the local priest can, for the most part, do very little. It is no good trying to exorcise something that you cannot see or understand, however much love you have in your heart. The other factor is that if you have a friendly ghost do send a tremendous amount of love out to them, for this will help greatly in their leaving the earth plane. No one needs to be attached to the earth because of fear or emotional trauma, and a good sensitive will merely discuss the situation with the entity and invite them to leave, and if this does not happen and the entity is causing problems then they can actually move them on according to spiritual law. Ghosts are simply displaced spirits who, rather like displaced persons, stay in one place until they can move to a permanent home. On the whole they are very rarely evil, and although haunting can be quite a traumatic event, it really is no more than a nuisance.

My personal experience of ghosts is quite extensive, and in our own home in Chelsea we helped a ghost who was a young housekeeper to find her freedom elsewhere. She was attached to the house because she had been murdered there. She was tied to the trauma of the murder, which in her case was strangulation, and had been unable to move away from the scene of the crime, down the stairs, outside to the river, where her body was dumped in the 1890s. Unfortunately for me, I forgot to persuade the murderer to go as well, and we had to repeat the process slightly more forcefully. As a result of the two ghosts departing the house has felt lighter, clearer and far more joyful than throughout the whole ten years I have lived there. This was a direct example of a delightfully loving, caring person who was a victim, and a particularly distasteful, evil character, who had actually committed the murder, not only of her but of several others as well.

Another experience happened when I recently stayed at Thornby Hall in Northamptonshire with my husband. During one afternoon I was asked by my host if I would take a look at a room that they had put by as a meditation room, but which he felt was extremely unhappy. Apparently it had been a bedroom, but no one had been able to sleep there and so they had emptied it of all the furniture except a chaise longue under the window. Peter and I entered the room, which was quite small with only this one piece of furniture in it, and immediately a presence, which was sitting on the chaise longue under the window, flew across the room to me and attached itself to me very firmly indeed. This was a young girl, very slim in a long, white dress. I sat down on the chaise longue and she channelled through me to Peter. She said she was a servant girl and had been in the house for only ten months. It was 1658 and she had been cleaning this room when the heavy wooden door slammed shut. The blast caused the fire to flare in the fireplace and her dress caught alight. Despite her agonizing screams no one could hear her as the walls were of thick stone. She tried to get out of the window, but the flames took hold too quickly and she burnt to death. The suffering in her voice was excrutiating and she didn't need to ask for our help. I asked her to stand up, and Peter and I held hands either side of her and simply willed her to go to her mother who was waiting for her. As Peter said, 'The energy shift was very evident' and there was a tremendous lightening in the room as the entity went. I left an amethyst crystal to absorb any remaining pain and suffering and after three days the room was really happy and could be used again.

Some ghosts have a really strong need and Sophia's story of the Green Lady illustrates this. Sophia says:

This took place at Lickleyhead Castle in Aberdeenshire in Scotland when my mother was about eleven. She was in her nursery, now the dining room, and this lady appeared to her in the window. She was a beautifully dressed lady in old-fashioned clothes and long green dress, and she was always pointing from the dining room down to the coal cellar. She appeared to my mother three or four times. My mother told my father because she knew he would understand. He said: 'Don't tell Mother, I'll have it looked into,' and a few years later they dug up the cellar and found a woman's bones as well as some other bones. They were taken off to Aberdeen University and checked and found to be human female bones. She must have spoken to my mother because she asked to be buried. So they had the bones taken off to the local cemetery and buried, and she never came back again.

Sarah's experience shows the possessiveness of spirits:

When I moved into my cottage in Brighton last year I felt several intermittent presences there and I quite often felt uncomfortable. It wasn't evil so much as I just felt there was somebody there who didn't particularly want me there, and it was quite strong at times and made me feel very uneasy. It was as if something came and went. The funny thing was that the times I didn't feel uncomfortable I felt very happy there and it was almost like one extreme to the other. When Tara came she saw that it was the previous owner who had suddenly and traumatically died and hadn't realized that, and wondered what on earth I was doing there. The other couple were an old man and a woman, also previous tenants, who liked my cat and recommended I bought a rocking chair! I eventually found my rocking chair and brought it back to the house with great glee, and it is now one of my most treasured possessions. I sit there and meditate in it.

Tara asked the first entity to be happy and leave the house, which she must have done as she has not been felt there since.

Famous ghosts include Jane Seymour who died in 1537 and Catherine Howard who died in 1542 at Hampton

Court. Also seen frequently is Anne Boleyn's ghost in the chapel in the Tower of London, and the ghost of Drury Lane, Dan Leno, who died in 1904. Others include the Duchess of Cleveland who died in 1710 in Chiswick Mall; Anne Chapman who died in 1888 in Hanbury Street, Spitalfields; the cripple in Hill Street, W1; and the Grey Lady in Wellington Barracks. All of these have been seen on many occasions by a diverse number of individuals who are sensitive enough to pick up their vibrations.

When is a ghost not a ghost? It is important not to confuse souls who are ghosts attached to the earth until they can be invited or persuaded to leave, and spirit guides or people who have passed on and died. Often a child will see a beloved grandparent who has passed on quite clearly and will have conversations with them. This is quite possible with parents too if they would only try!

The link between someone who dies and the living is one of *love* when this happens.

Gods and Goddesses

Gods are the supreme beings, of masculine and feminine nature, that are said to have power over nature and human fortunes. In nearly every religion in the world God is seen as the supreme being, the creator and ruler of the universe. In mystical religions, in India, China and the Far East, the image of God is an abstraction because it is still and yet moves. It depends on nothing yet supplies the needs of everything. This supreme God, therefore, could not be put in any form and many personal and localized images came into being so that people could communicate with the supreme God through an intermediary. In prophetic religions in the Near East, Europe and the Americas, there is the belief that there is a personal God who rules the universe and speaks to men through prophets and law givers. This

God is seen as being personally concerned with the way the world should be run, even though He is also seen as eternal and exempt from all the conditions of time and space. It can be seen, therefore, that the idea of a supreme power or God is the way that man, who represents the microcosmos, can relate to God, who represents the macrocosmos.

The idea that man needs the intermediary state has led to thousands of manifestations of that one God. In India Krishna is seen as a supreme personality of godhead. He plays the same role as Jesus does in Christian beliefs, as the words he speaks are considered to be words direct from the Supreme God. In Egyptian mythology Ra is seen as the soul of the sun, the source of divine descent. In Greek mythology Zeus was the father of gods and men, seen to be the most powerful of all immortals. He was the sky deity whose presence was marked by lightning and thunder. His wife, who was also his sister, was Hera, the patroness of marriage. Other gods in mythology include Aphrodite, goddess of love and fertility, born from the sea; her Roman counterpart is Venus. Eros was the son of Aphrodite and is the god of love. Apollo represents the ideal of manly duty, while Hades was the Greek god of the underworld, sometimes called Pluto. Neptune is the Roman god of water, and Pan the Greek god of flocks and herds, represented as half goat and half man. Artemis was a primitive earth goddess but she appears in Greek mythology as the daughter of Zeus and Leto, the virgin huntress and patroness of chastitity. Athene was the patron goddess of Athens and was supposed to have sprung fully grown and armed from the head of Zeus. Dionysus is the God of inspiration and ecstasy and represents the irrational impulses of human nature.

The idea that there is one God who looks over lesser deities is present in all practices. In Africa the Supreme God may have hundreds of different names but they all have one thing in common. The Supreme God is considered to be the master of the world and master of human destiny. Under his rule are all the lesser godlings, each with their own special function. His lesser gods make it possible to approach God with personal requests and needs. This idea is not confined to paganism for Christians often approach God through the Virgin, the apostles or saints and martyrs. In the Moslem religion, Mohammed and his fellow prophets act as buffers between man and God. Therefore, the lesser 'Gods' represent both a barrier and a stepping stone between the individual human and the Infinite.

Graphology

This has developed more recently into quite an art, as handwriting is a reflection of your character and personality. A graphologist needs six or seven lines of your usual handwriting and studies how you approach your words and letters. Do they begin with straight or curved strokes? Is the stroke long or short? The angle, length and pressure of the stroke shows how independent you are, how quickly you think and the way you deal with people and situations. More and more people are relying on this art, particularly those who write in for jobs to large companies. Graphology is literally able to provide character references. When I was about twelve I read a book on graphology and discovered that curves and loops showed that you had tremendous generosity and open-mindedness. As my handwriting was still in its formative stage I immediately adopted gracious curves and loops everywhere. Luckily most of them have now been dropped!

Grimoires

Grimoires are verses or statements full of symbolic language giving information on the hierarchy of spirits and demons; describing their form and giving instructions on how to conjure them up. The most famous grimoire is the 'Key of Solomon', which gives details of the appearance and quality of seventy-two spirits in the Nether Region which were invoked by King Solomon. The instructions given in grimoires are very precise and they can easily conjure up powerful spirits or demons.

In the teachings of the past, knowledge was transmitted from generation to generation by word of mouth, from master to student, or if written down was kept very secret. Later the sacred books provided an exterior form of knowledge, while the secret knowledge was only passed on to initiates. In the Middle Ages these secrets started to be released in the form of grimoires. These were a mixture of Persian, Hebrew, Christian and magical literature mixed with absurd and childish nonsense. Most of the information contained in grimoires is very dangerous to the undisciplined mind, because it exposes you to energies that have a tremendous force and therefore need to be channelled properly, or it turns on the person that has evoked it, causing destruction and confusion. Even reading some of them can have an immediate effect, so leave them alone unless you are under a wise and knowledgeable teacher.

Guru

The age of the Guru is long past, and as the Aquarian Age dawns you will find that you are your own guru and need no other. In the last two thousand years spiritual teachers have popped up in most continents and often are self-styled masters. They collect their pupils around them and teach them what to believe as their own truth. With the Aquarian Age, this type of teaching is no longer necessary for the spiritual teacher of today will teach the pupil that they are the master and only provide them with tools and techniques to find out their own truth. Everyone's experience of life is individual and no one sees life through anyone else's spectacles anymore. The greatest teaching you can receive is how to stay in your heart centre, how to follow your intuition and rely upon it. No longer do we sit at the feet of the master. We are always responsible for our own development, thoughts and actions, and no one can change this. It is possible for you to stay within your heart centre and to feel rather than think. It is also possible for you to follow your own path and your own destiny helped by the knowledge that those who can point you in the right direction will appear in your life at the right time. Do not listen to false prophets, but listen to your own heart, for it is only there that you can find the truth.

Hallucination

Hallucinations can occur to anyone and you don't have to be suffering from a mental illness or be seriously disturbed to have one. It is simply a visual misinterpretation of the senses. In other words, it is something that is not actually happening that you think is happening; so whether you hear something that isn't there or see something that doesn't exist or even sense something that isn't real, it is all hallucination. All our senses can easily be foiled and tricked in everyday life, particularly if you take hallucinogens which are drugs which produce hallucinations. Although these experiences are often vivid, they can also be traumatic and have a very serious effect on the psyche. Hallucinations can also be induced by suggestion in a hypnotized subject, so this is something else to be very, very careful about. An hallucination is not an illusion but it is a perception which has no objective basis.

Hallucinogens

Hallucinogens are drugs which have been used in all cultures and in all ages to develop telepathic sensitivity and psychic ability.

In one example, in 1502 at the coronation of Montezuma II, the Aztec ruler of Mexico, a feast of pickled mushrooms caused the guests to have visions, to become instantly psychic and to have premonitions of the future. Others committed suicide. Certain types of mushrooms and cacti are most often used, together with LSD, hashish and mescalin, which not only induce visions but also mark changes in perception and thought process, and abrupt changes in behaviour. Any drug taken in massive doses will induce delirium, hallucinatins and frenzy, for drugs alter the biochemistry of the brain.

There is no doubt that drugs such as these do arouse psychic abilities but in an unregulated and chaotic way and not without several undesirable physical side-effects. No one in their right mind would try to develop their psyche in this way for it is rather like forcing a flower to open when it is in bud. Once forced open you'll find it impossible to shut down again. It will take an adept to rectify such damage, if at all. Psychic ability is your birthright and the ability to hear clearly, see clearly and feel clearly will develop in its own way or with a teacher who understands your particular rhythm. Forcing your centres open can only be harmful and have very short-term value. The answer is, *don't*.

During the sixties when flower-power was the rage and the new generation of peace lovers started looking inside themselves rather than outside themselves for answers, hallucinogens came into fashion. I have had to exorcize two people who have taken LSD, forced their psychic centres open and been unable to close them down again. It caused nightmares and a great deal of fear. One of them said, 'I'm completely out of control and it is very frightening.'

Haunting

Ghosts haunt people and places and this is because they are stuck in time and space and have nowhere to go and nothing else to do. Being earth-bound spirits of the dead they generally haunt the place where they died, if they had a violent death, and most of them had; or they hover around over a pot of money buried in the floor because they're avaricious; or they wail, walking along beside some tragedy that is yet to be solved. Haunting can be terribly boring and the best way to clear it up is to talk to the ghost quietly and calmly and suggest that they move on. Being stuck in space and time is no joke and unless someone has the sympathy and love to do this sort of work, these earth-bound spirits are in limbo. Headless figures stalking around the battlements of an ancient castle on the night of a full moon are very much a thing of the past and anyone enlightened and caring enough should hold themselves personally responsible to end the whole fiasco. It's true that anywhere can be haunted: it doesn't have to be an ancient castle, a ruined abbey or the Tower of London. You can even find haunted bingo halls, council houses and shops. I recently moved the ghost caretaker out of a building that is my hairdresser's. He was simply stuck there because he loved his job and loathed his wife and thought he'd be happier at his work base than with his wife wherever she was. Hauntings take all sorts of different forms and you can see glowing lights or flashes or sparks, or you can hear voices or footsteps and squeaky doors. Walking into certain rooms that are colder than other rooms in a house also indicates the haunting presence of a ghost; also the ghost can touch you and you'll feel it.

I had two ghosts in my own house in Chelsea: a murderer and the victim. When we discovered this my husband and I approached the victim, a young seventeen-year-old housekeeper; it took us three days to help her on her way. As she was strangled after being raped, I had to go through an approximation of her demise in order to help her release herself. Mind you, not everyone's willing to do this or capable of it. She also had a marvellous trick of being able to switch my bedside lamp on and off when she felt she couldn't cope with the situation. She did appear to us some three months after she left the house to say how very happy she was with her parents and thanked us for our trouble.

It is very dangerous indeed for the amateur to try to move a ghost on; that is to exorcize. It is much safer to ask someone who understands and who can see clearly what is happening. On the other hand, I would never advise you to run away from a ghost unless you feel it is downright evil. Most ghosts are really 'stuck' and are desperate to communicate. By simply standing your ground and offering a hand of friendship, even though your heart may be beating a mile a minute, makes a lot more sense and is a far more loving approach. Explaining to people that they really are dead is often all that is required and then they can be helped on to where they need to go. Because they can see, hear and feel everything that's going on around them and have everything except a physical body it is often very difficult for certain people to realize they've died, particularly if it was extremely sudden or violent. So offer a helping hand if you feel there is a ghost near you. If you feel extremely uncomfortable or have a sense of evil then please, please refer the matter to someone who understands. Ghosts aren't there for amusement and they're not there as a public spectacle. They are genuinely stuck in time and space and genuinely need to be helped on.

Healing

Faith healing or spiritual healing is usually resorted to by those who have found that all other methods have failed. What a tragedy this is, as everyone is a healer and we all remember our grandparents and parents soothing us when we cut a finger or fell down and grazed our knee, by rubbing the spot and cleaning out the wound, cuddling us and making us feel good. This is faith healing in its simplest form. My grandfather Henry used to put his hand on my head when I had a headache and I always felt better for it, for it was a simple transfer of energy. His positive force replaced my negative one and I felt better from the contact. Contrary to the belief of many people, you do not need to have faith to be faith-healed for everyone is a healer and everyone is capable of healing themselves.

The body is indeed the temple of the soul and it is up to you to look after your diet and to exercise to keep yourself fit and to dress sensibly whatever the weather. Your body is very important and is not a machine as you will find out if you overstretch it in any direction, or overwork it, skipping sleep and rest and expecting it to perform endless tasks at all times. The body is however, like a machine in that when it is pushed to its limit it can break down or collapse altogether. Certain parts can rust or simply fail to perform in their normally smooth way. Looking after yourself is the first aspect of healing. With today's interest in wholefoods and alternative medicine, the answer is at hand.

If you feel you need help, then go to a healer with whom you feel comfortable. If there is warmth and caring in the voice, a genuine concern and sincerity, you have probably found the person who is right for you. The first question any good healer asks is, 'May I heal this person?' If you have drawn illness or an accident to yourself for a reason then no one has any right whatsoever to interfere with the process. They certainly wouldn't be doing you any favour if they did. This may sound strange, but we actually learn and grow through suffering and through discomfort. When I was young, my mother was repeatedly in hospital with several major operations and I was the one elected to go and visit her some ten miles away, a long bus ride. There was never anyone, I'm sure, so bored silly as I was. I bitterly resented spending sunny Saturdays making the long trek, the smell of disinfectant and those long, long corridors with their endless stretches of linoleum, the squeak of wheelchair wheels and the inevitable grapes and fresh clothing. Yes, I loved my mother but I spent so much time visiting the hospital that I resented her illness and the time it took out of my own life.

The result of this experience over several years made me become very intolerant of people who were ill and I had little patience or concern for them. Compassion was not a word that I understood. I simply didn't want to know. In my late twenties I developed an incurable disease of the spine called osteocondritis, the fusing of the vertebrae. It was so painful that, for almost a year, the only relief I had was lying flat on the ground. I suffered almost constant pain through most of that time. For nine months I worked with a healer to right it, as orthodox medicine gave me up for lost and doctors told me I should take cortisone for life. I refused to touch it and sought other ways. Eventually, it dawned on me that, as I became more compassionate towards myself and more caring about my own body, so I could develop compassion for others who were similarly hurt and ailing. When this took root, I was cured. It had taken exactly a year of my life. Within two weeks I started healing myself and have been doing it ever since. It is important to realize that what you draw to you is what you need and to look at every accident and every illness, even the common cold, and ask yourself, 'What is going on with me?' Nothing happens by chance and everything happens for a reason. One of the most common complaints of people who do a certain form of meditation with me is that they have streaming colds or even the 'flu during the process. This is a complete cleansing on the physical level as they stretch themselves spiritually to gain a foothold in the higher realms. It never fails.

To become a healer is very simple. You simply have to be able to love another human being and to feel compassion: like Mother Theresa in Calcutta, dressing a leper's wounds, thinking not of her own comfort. No amount of training in the world can get you to love another human being so you are a healer through your own love and not through any methods offered to you. No amount of waving the hands through the aura or wearing a white coat and socks will make you a healer.

There are two main ways that the healing function operates. One is through your own magnetism and your own power and energy through love and the other is by opening yourself up to the cosmic force which pours through you through the crown of your head and manifests through the hands. You will find when you start healing and ask for this force to come through you that your hands can get very hot and seem to enlarge; this also happens on the subtle level. I always make the person who has come to see me work as hard as I do; they need to visualize colour and visualize wellness in the part that is affected. They also have to find out why it has all come about. Otherwise, I am merely a Mr Fixit and the whole session is wasted. Unless you *learn* from the experience you will only have it again another time, perhaps even worse.

With more love in our lives, most illness, unless it is karmic in origin, can be cured. I was reading recently about a survey conducted on a very wide sample of men who suffered from heart attacks and coronary troubles. Over 90 per cent of them had difficulty in expressing emotion and couldn't talk about their feelings. It is literally this hardening of the heart that causes the heart to stop and it is only by love and the giving and receiving of love that such problems can be solved. Can you love another human being? Then you are a healer.

Heaven and Hell

Myself am Hell;
And, in the lowest deep, a lower deep,
Still threat'ning to devour me, opens wide;
To which the Hell I suffer seems a Heaven.

John Milton
Paradise Lost

Most religions preach about heaven and hell and many of us have been brought up with the idea that, when we die, we will either go to a place of bliss and light, which is heaven, or we'll sink through our own iniquities and sins to the fiery furness, complete with demons and devils with pitch forks, screaming and gnashing of teeth, which is hell. Do you really believe this? The myth of heaven and hell must be the most extraordinary one, for there is no such thing.

You make your own heaven right now on planet earth, or you can make your own hell, it is entirely up to you. Life can be hell for many people for, through negative thinking and disruptive thoughts, they can surround themselves with jealousy, anger, greed and discontentment. By not nurturing your own spirit you can be in hell, by living entirely for material things and finding no comfort at the end of the day, you can be in hell, or simply by taking everything and giving nothing, you can be in hell. You not only can be in hell, yourself, you can create if for other people by the way you live and the quality of your living. Have you made someone happy today or have you, by your own thoughts and actions, created a very unpleasant and difficult situation for them? A word of praise is so much more valuable than criticism.

Creating your own heaven can be a wonderful and fulfilling experience. Start the day with a smile and be determined that you will flow with events without forcing your will on others. Being in heaven is leading a loving and caring life, taking great joy in everything and helping those less fortunate than yourself. Being in heaven means knowing how to love without being possessive, jealous or clinging. It means loving without thought of return.

So what happens when you die if you believe in heaven and hell? The answer is that you'll get exactly what you think you're going to get. If you have no beliefs at all, then you'll just go through the natural order of things, but if you do believe that you will go to hell through your misdeeds, sins and misdemeanours, then you'll probably have a vision of that. Those who imagine heaven to be a place where angels sit on clouds playing harps all day and singing songs, will probably find that. There have been reported cases of arriving in such a state and gradually noticing that the angels look very weary and have dust on their wings and their harps are not quite in tune! It is all what you expect and create for yourself. You can create everything for yourself, for that is your great ability and magnificent gift. Which will you choose on planet earth. Heaven or hell?

Hex

This is another word for the practice of witchcraft; the name Hexer or Hexse means wizard or witch. Witchcraft is found all over the world and widely believed in Germany, Britain and in many areas of the United States, especially Pennsylvania. To hex a person means to inflict evil upon them by magic or witchcraft and is a word in common usage in the American language. It is very similar to the practice of the evil eye.

Holy Grail

The Holy Grail dates back into mythology and was a pre-Christian Celtic symbol now disguised and kept alive in the trappings of Christianity. The real grail bearer is supposed to be a pagan god called Bran, who in ancient Celtic myth, was the possessor of a magical cauldron capable of bringing people back to life. The grail itself was then conceived in later Christian documents as a large dish which contained many magical powers. Only later did it become the cup used by Christ to perform the rites of the Last Supper. The dish was rescued from Pontius Pilate by Jesus's uncle, Joseph of Arimathea, and was brought to Britain as a sacred talisman. It was then buried or lost in Glastonbury and was not found until the appearance of Sir Percival, one of King Arthur's knights, who found the grail and underwent many spiritual trials in order to understand its powers. By this time it was not only regarded as a Christian relic but also as a magical vessel that could show its owners all the secrets and knowledge of the universe. The grail has been lost ever since King Arthur's day; it has been sought by scholars and occultists ever since.

Another famous grail romance involved the Templars, the German version of the guardian of the grail. They were a kind of military police protecting the pilgrims travelling to and from Jerusalem. The knights took vows of poverty, chastity and obedience, but eventually became incredibly rich, outlived their usefulness and were believed to worship an idol called Bathomet. Eventually they were all arrested and tortured.

Almost every cult and religion has its chalice and its own symbolic meaning, but the principle and the message is always the same. Font, bowl, cup or chalice contains the water of life and everyone has the right to drink of it to the full. The grail represents the magical power of renewed life, providing all material needs and also giving all known knowledge, power and wisdom. It is thought that, if you saw the grail on any day, you would be immune to death the following week and your looks would never change for two hundred years, apart from your hair going grey. The grail symbolizes the search for immortality and wisdom and I believe that it is already in our hearts. Only seek and you will find.

Hypnosis

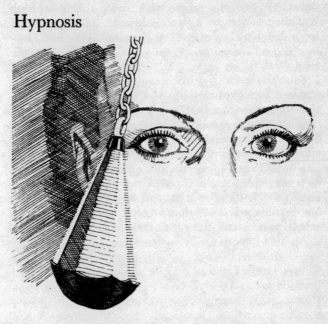

The word comes from the Greek 'God of Sleep'; however, the hypnotic state is not sleep at all and medical science cannot define it as a separate consciousness. A large proportion of people cannot be hypnotized or put into a trance of any kind. This is usually because there is a strong mental block formed in early childhood. At the beginning, it was thought that no one could be forced to do something that was against their beliefs or moral standards, but this has been found not to be the case.

Hypnosis is a valuable tool used by spy rings to collect intelligence information. In the middle of the Second World War a professor of psychology at Colgate University, USA, announced that he could hypnotize anyone, without their knowledge or consent, into committing treason against the USA. Frightening indeed! Yet the good news about hypnotism is that it can help with phobias, smoking, diet and sexual problems. Childbirth, bone setting and even the pain of toothache and extraction have all been successfully side-tracked into trance conditions. Hypnosis can be used as an anaesthetic in cases of surgery.

The power of hypnosis can be demonstrated by someone with an allergy which is, after all, simply a basic biochemical reaction. Or is it? Under hypnosis, someone suffering an allergy from eating strawberries could be told that he was eating some other fruit and would not appear to have the allergy. As long as he was told that it was a different fruit, nothing happened. Hypnosis can even get rid of warts in certain cases. But we still do not know enough about hypnosis; all we know is that we do not use anything other than a very small fraction of our mental powers and that a little knowledge is a dangerous thing.

I Ching

I Ching represents one of the first efforts of the human mind to consider and understand all the forces that form the structure of the universe. This ancient Chinese philosophy was based on the idea that the physical universe is a combination of the dark, feminine, passive forces of matter, and the light, masculine, creative forces. These two forces are known as Yin, seen as a broken line, and Yang, the male solid line. Different combinations of these principles are represented by sixty-four hexagrams which were conceived to represent all that happens in the physical and spiritual planes. The alternations between Yin-Yang produce change and result in all the diversity of the universe and every condition in our life. Therefore, each hexagram describes a series of changes that can show the inquirer what is, what has been and what is to come.

I Ching is closely associated with the Tao, the way things work in the universal order of things. It is believed that there are certain patterns of natural spontaneity that you can either flow with or go against. By moving with the natural flow of things your life has a path with the least resistance, by not flowing you incur obstacles and things that you cannot deal with. This brings about frustration, misunderstanding and sufferings. *I Ching*, therefore, gives you the chance to look at the patterns that surround you so that you can assess what the present situation is, how you got there and what appropriate action you should take so that you will be able to go forward. This is not as easy or as straightforward as it sounds, because the *I Ching* talks of the superior man! This is an image of someone who is capable of flowing with the Tao; most of us not only do not do this, but will find it hard to see things from that perspective.

Discovery of the trigrams, composed of any combination of three sides of broken lines are attributed to Pao Hsi, a mythical figure who is said to have been the first Emperor of China. The way the trigrams were devised is described in one of the commentaries on the *I Ching*; in ancient times, when Pao Hsi ruled all things under heaven, he looked up and contemplated the bright patterns of the sky then looked down and considered the shapes of the earth.

He noted the decorative markings on birds and beasts and the appropriate qualities of their territories. Close at hand, he studied his own body and also observed distant things. From all this he devised the eight trigrams in order to unveil the heavenly processes in nature and to understand the character of everything.

The eight trigrams represent the different combinations of the masculine and feminine character. At a later date, the trigrams were formed into more combinations by Wei, a powerful feudal lord who lived in the second century. He combined the trigrams into a combination of six lines to form hexagrams with a total of sixty-four in all, which he named and for which he provided an explanatory test. His son added the commentaries and in the fifth century Confucius studied the book and added a further commentary. The six lines that make up a hexagram are either solid or broken; these form the forces that either combine like the sun and rain (to germinate the seed and bring about growth), or are seen in combat like fire and water (which both try to gain supremacy over each other). *I Ching* took the family unit, the seasons and the elements to describe all the flows of change in the universe.

The simplest way to use the *I Ching* as an oracle is to use three coins to determine the shape of the trigrams. Before throwing the coins you decide which side of the coin is going to represent the Yang and which the Yin principle. If heads is chosen to symbolize Yin, a coin toss of two heads and one tail will symbolize a Yin line and should be put down on paper as the bottom line of the hexagram. The toss of two tails and one head will mean a Yang line. Three heads will mean an old Yin line, which will be converted into Yang lines, forming a new design and thus a new hexagram. On the other hand the toss of three tails will symbolize an old Yang line which will result in a new Yin line and thus in a new hexagram. The coins are thrown six times to determine each line. The position of the lines has a distinct significance. The bottom line, the first to be drawn, means the body, the middle line represents the mind and the top corresponds to the soul. The other method of casting a hexagram involves the use of fifty yarrow stalks between one and two feet long. Many serious readers of the book see the coin method as a lazy alternative and prefer the complicated method using the yarrow sticks because it forms a type of ceremony and creates the right mood of reverence and detachment. The fall of yarrow sticks or coin will reflect what your situation is at that particular moment. An example of this can be seen if we take the hexagram K'un, the receptive earth:

K'un represents the nature of earth, strong in devotion. Among the seasons it stands for late autumn when all the forces of life are at rest. If this came up for you it may mean that your own inner strength will sustain you and you need to wait before any action can be taken. If, in three months' time, you did the *I Ching* again you might get the hexagram Fu, return, which represents thunder, the movement that stirs anew within the earth at the time of the solstice. It symbolizes the return of life, therefore this change can be interpreted as a very good sign for which your patience has paid off. Fu shows that it is a good time to put all your energy into new projects or a time to approach old problems in a new way. It is a characteristic of the *I Ching* that it gives a cut-and-dried answer.

The *I Ching* can be consulted as an oracle or a book of wisdom. As an oracle you can become aware of a situation in the early stages and, by taking the right action, avoid unnecessary conflict and suffering. As a book of wisdom it is unsurpassed because it shows the workings and reasons for change and exposes the reader to the deepest levels of intuitive knowledge and insight. Jung believed that the symbols and words contained in the *I Ching* conveyed messages direct to the unconscious mind.

Illusions

Illusions are not objective but are places or objects that have been wrongly perceived. A conjuror produces illusions through the tricks of his trade to mystify the senses. Illusions are not hallucinations which is all imagination or mass hypnosis.

Many people over periods of time have seen phantom scenery: lakes, castles, houses and even ships that appear and disappear and which cannot be located subsequently. Some of the documented cases are certainly tricks of light or perhaps hallucinations but others can not be explained by atmospheric changes or some such thing.

The writer Barbara Cartland and her brother came upon 'a storybook castle with spires and turrets', while walking in the countryside in southern Austria near

Carinthia. When they got back to the local village and talked about what they had seen they were told that the castle had long ago been destroyed.

There is no doubt that the universe may be infinitely more cluttered than we can perceive or dare imagine, and besides ghosts of people and animals there are ghosts of buildings. One of the strangest ghostly legends of all time is the *Flying Dutchman*, a ship without a crew but with a single skeleton on board. The ship's captain, Cornelius Vanderdecken, accused God of becalming and obstructing his ship's passage. He swore that, if it took him until the Day of Judgment, he would not be thwarted and he would not round the Cape. God obviously took the blasphemous captain at his word and to this day he still sails the Seven Seas! In 1881 twelve şailors on HMS *Bacchante* saw the *Flying Dutchman* in all its eerie ghostliness. The ship was sailing from Melbourne to Sidney at the time. The full description was recorded in the ship's log. Interestingly enough, the officer of the watch who wrote the log up was, at the time, the Duke of York, later to become King George VI.

Infinity

To see a world in a grain of sand,
And a heaven in a wild flower:
Hold infinity in the palm of your hand
And eternity in an hour.

William Blake
Auguries of Innocence

The symbol for infinity is ∞ and is beyond our imagination, being something greater than any quantity that we can possibly think of. It is usually associated with the idea of the Creator, for it is deemed that He is the positive and negative, creative and passive, and the universe is the harmonious union of perfect opposites, equal in strength and perfection. He knows the true meaning of harmony for He is harmony within himself. It is thought that man is made in the image of the Creator; therefore it is reasonable to assume that we have that quality and infinity and it is our destiny to find and realize that quality within ourselves so that we may also find perfect harmony and balance.

Initiation

Initiation is a point of time in moving from one level of consciousness to another. It marks the stepping stones, rather like the steps at the side of a pyramid, of a soul's journey through various stages of knowledge and wisdom.

Initiation in the past often meant elaborate ritual and ceremony, but today it is much, much simpler. The Egyptians perfected the initiation ceremony and it is thought that Moses, Jesus Christ and St Paul gained much wisdom through the Essenes. Today, the Egyptian ceremonies are still practised, although in a very different form, by freemasons, Rosicrucians and some Christian Churches. Philosophers such as Plato, Cicero and Pythagoras were also Egyptian initiates. So what really happened?

The Great Pyramid has always been regarded as an Initiation Temple. After a great deal of preparation the candidate was placed in the great stone coffer in the King's chamber. The lid was put on and for three days his spirit could wander through the various planes of existence. The candidate knew that his body was merely a vehicle and that the soul could travel and return without death. If the candidate survived the three days and didn't go insane or hysterical then he was declared an initiate.

Today we no longer do this, although the number

three still has its significance. The initiations that I have experienced, and those who are close to me have experienced, have been major turning points of understanding and knowledge. Each one has altered the personality and affected thinking patterns and actions. It is very like standing on a step of the Great Pyramid and looking up to the next one knowing that is where you need to be. The distance of the step looks enormous from where you are standing and you can see no way of climbing it or of getting up there, yet suddenly you are there and you can look back and look up to the next one. I believe there are twelve initiations which lead to mastership.

The first initiation occurs at around seven years of age. As you come out of this childhood phase, intense energies stimulate the mind, increasing intellect and awareness. More physical energies come into play at puberty and, when you get to the age of twenty-one, you enter into the adult phase. This is an initiation when your intellectual and physical abilities are at full strength, and you're able to project more strongly than before. In most countries there is an initiation ceremony and it is taken very seriously but, in the western world, it is just a party and a joyful celebration. It will mean a great deal if you realize the significance of this age and you may well come across initiation processes when you are subject to intense energies. By accepting these and moving through them, you will be able to see and feel a great many things, increasing your own learning and knowledge. Even when you start to work in the world, there is an initiation process. When you start your college education or to to university, or when you start a job, then you're initiated into the energies of that job and these can take many forms.

When you die you are initiated into another world and, for some of you, this may be the greatest initiation that you can ever have, if you're in a conscious state when this occurs.

Intuition

Intuition happens when you don't think consciously. It is the inner sense by which we always know the difference between right and wrong. Intuition always come instantly and spontaneously without reasoning or logical thought. How many times have you had a hunch or a strange feeling that you ought to do something without anyone telling you? Perhaps you have simply known which job to take out of two or three. There are so many incidences in our everyday life that we deal with intuitively. Choosing a new outfit or new hair style can be intuitive. It is simply knowing. Sometimes you will be aware of what someone is going to say before they say it, or anticipate a person entering a room or leaving before they do so. This is the intuitive faculty at work.

If you make your decisions with the intuitive part of your mind you very seldom go wrong. The intuition is based in the heart centre and the heart centre cannot lie. A rational and logical mind can cause much chaos and confusion for it is often faulty, relying as it does on imperfect experience or education. The heart centre, or intuitive centre, relies on deep inner knowing only. It is only when the mind gets in the way that we tend to make bad decisions. How many times have you reacted strongly against someone you have just met but have tried to rationalize that that person cannot be really that difficult or really so aggressive or really so manipulative? Yet, later on, your intuitive sense is proved right. First impressions are *always* right so learn to trust them.

The key to happy living is to learn to trust your intuition. It has taken me many years to make a decision entirely from the heart centre, for the mind continually tries to get in on the act. One of the ways I teach is awareness of where your consciousness is at any given moment. Sit with your eyes shut and your hand physically on your heart, and allow yourself to feel your consciousness in the head, and slowly sense it moving

114

downwards to the third eye, between the eyebrows and further still, down to the throat and yet further still until your consciousness is right beneath your hand in the heart chakra. When you have visualized this, allow yourself a moment to feel the heart beat and to know that this is the area from which your decision will be made. If someone has a very well-developed intellect it takes practice to trust this very simple yet effective method. Every few minutes you tend to go back to the head and have to repeat this exercise and practise it many times. Yet it is the most wonderful exercise to experiment with. Live intuitively and you'll live life with far less mistakes and more certainty.

Invocation

The most well-known invocation in the West is the Lord's Prayer. When you say it out loud or in your mind you're invoking the energy of the Cosmic Christ Force to assist you in your life, or to help with any problems. Everyone invokes some force when someone is dangerously ill or if there has been some terrible accident in the family. The occultist will probably invoke the particular earth energies or maybe even planetary ones that they understand and can control. It is necessary to make sure that, when you do invoke something, you're capable of controlling it or correcting it, or you may find that the force has a disruptive effect instead of a constructive one. If the invocation is done with sincerity and deliberation, the effects can be quite dramatic and instantaneous. Obviously, what you're asking for should be in the realm of possibility because otherwise you end up forcing the issue and breaking apart all the love and constructive energy that surrounds the problem. Most invocations are in the form of prayers and these are constructed so that you call for help from the heart; selfish invocations get the mind and the ego grasping and pushing for help.

A few years ago two friends of mine were driving back from the pub very drunk. They went round a sharp bend and the car ploughed into a shop front. The driver was only bruised but the passenger was badly injured and had a blood clot that slowly moved towards his brain. He was put on the critical list and during the following twenty-four hours it would be known whether he would live or die. The driver went home with his wife, feeling guilty and sad. They both stayed up all night praying from their heart, and hoping that he would get better. By mid-morning they had heard that the blood clot had moved past the brain, causing no damage and that he was off the danger list. Did the prayers or invocation have any effect at all? Who is to say? True love, and constructive thought is a much better thing to send to someone than worry or self-indulgence.

Jewels and Crystals

Crystals have been described as 'The flowers of the Mineral Kingdom'. Their rare beauty and shining faces have made them prized among the dowdier examples of the mineral realm.

Gems begin as crystals and are shaped to give sparkle. Certain types of crystal have been prized as ornaments for thousands of years. Not only that, but in ancient times they were thought to have certain powers and were valued as amulets and talismans. The more modern view of gems and crystals gives them less power but there is, nonetheless, a certain special quality to them that defies rational explanation.

Crystals are formed in hollows or cavities in the earth's surface, and grow from natural solutions. They grow as their atoms arrange themselves in specialized patterns, with differing outer forms. The same inner patterns also cause crystals to behave very differently from one another when subjected to various types of energy. The energy field produced by a human being, the aura, interacts with the pattern of the crystal, causing it to respond to human energy. Because everyone is different, and has a slightly different energy pattern, crystals produce a wide range of responses. They are often used in healing and meditation, and people who own them often feel an attraction, almost akin to friendship, passing between themselves and their crystals. I certainly love the crystals I have.

All the rocks that make up the earth are made either from crystals or ground up pieces of crystal, so when you hold a crystal in your hands, you are holding a piece of the living earth. Many sensitives can even feel the natural rhythms of the earth, just by holding the crystal. Crystals were used in the great temples of Atlantis, and it was partly through their misuse in Atlantis that it was lost. The growing interest in crystals world-wide today is part of a re-awakening of knowledge from early times, except that this time there is a great impulse to get it right!

In choosing and using crystals, it is important to work from an inner sense of what feels right, and to use your intuition. The subtle energies of the crystal are unseen by the thinking mind but are easily sensed through the feeling mind so you should always choose crystals that you feel drawn to, regardless of what you have read or heard about them. Many people believe that there is a connection between their astrological sign and a certain crystal in the form of a birth stone; this is not true. The whole concept of birth stones is an invention of the jewellery trade and changes frequently depending on which gems are readily available! So, forget that you are Aquarius, Taurus or Libra, and that you have read that you should have such and such a stone – just simply go for whatever you feel drawn to, and it will always be the right one. Often closing your eyes and simply holding two crystals in your hands helps you decide.

Crystals respond to human will or intention and can be programmed for good or for ill. There is no doubt there are many cursed jewels around and perhaps the story of the Hope diamond is the most famous. Whoever wore the Hope diamond brought disaster or misfortune to themselves and their family. Crystals are very powerful indeed and can attract negativity or positivity. If the jewel has attracted or been programmed to negativity, then misfortune is bound to occur. I saw the Hope diamond recently in a museum in Washington DC and approached it with caution. It should be full of love and light now. So make sure that your intention produces no harm, either to yourself, to anyone else, or to the earth. Of course, it is a good idea to have this intention with *everything* you undertake, whether it involves crystals or not!

Using the crystal involves being sensitive both to yourself and to the crystal, and also to the world around you. If you wish to create peace and harmony in a particular situation, the crystal can have great harmonizing influences. If you are ill, or recovering from an injury, the crystal can have great healing powers. Working with a crystal can be as easy as just holding it in your hand, and seeing a picture in your mind of what you wish to happen, and asking the crystal to help you bring it about. But, before you do anything, be sure to read the section on Spiritual Law, and be certain that everything you do with crystals follows those natural laws. Otherwise, unintentional harm can result.

I work with crystals all the time, and find tremendous joy and comfort from them.

Kirlian Photography

Kirlian photography shows the energy flow or energy body around, say, a hand, or around any plant, animal or rock. The name 'Kirlian' comes from the inventor and

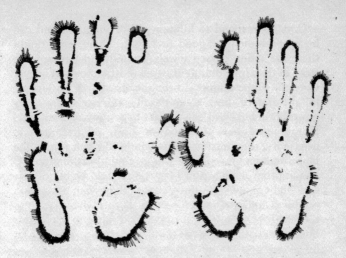

the apparatus uses a very high-frequency electric current passing between metal plates. The aura that surrounds all living things is then photographed.

It is a good experiment to have your hands photographed then do some healing on someone and have them photographed again. Your hands will certainly show a marked difference in the energy field. The photographs also pick up your physical and emotional state. Even if you photograph your hand, then kiss your sweetheart and have it photographed again it will be different! Kirlian photography can also be used by the healer, particularly photographs of the hand, to find out what is going on in the body. You will see from the picture that certain parts of the fingers seem to have a brighter force-field than others and a much stronger aura. Each finger has a particular meaning and if you have a lot of black dots appearing on your photograph, then this shows your body is full of poisons which need to be eliminated by careful diet. It is also a wonderful help to see how you are progressing along the spiritual path. Having your hands photographed once a year is quite an indication of progress or not!

Knots

Most people no longer remember the significance of the knot, for knots represent the sealed bargain. In the past, the merchant would tie a cord around his waist to indicate the deal made, and the monks, friars and nuns used to knot the cords around their waists in a special way, signifying their religious commitment. In symbolism, the continuous knot takes the form of a horizontal figure eight representing infinity. In mysticism it was thought that, if you were to untie a knot to its heart, you would have solved a mystery within yourself. Alexander cut the Gordian Knot which was tied so intricately, that no one could undo, and it became a symbol of his power, as he was seen as the true conqueror of the East. In many secret societies and religious orders, knotting and binding took place during initiation. These are symbolic gestures, but psychologically, they represent the idea that you are *bound* to do good on certain levels.

Kundalini

Kundalini comes from the Sanskrit word meaning 'something coiled' – a snake or a rope. It is also the vital and vitalizing force that lies dormant at the base of the spine. Through various yoga techiniques it can be aroused and will shoot up the spine, rising through the six chakras. As it does so, there is a tremendous increase of self-awareness and intensification of each energy centre. Psychic awareness and spiritual awakening usually follow. There is great danger, however, in raising the kundalini power too soon. I had a friend who did just this; he was an expert at yoga but he was not spiritually ready and had a nervous breakdown for over a year. If the energy centres are awakened quickly, the kundalini or serpent fire rises uncontrollably up the chakras or psychic centres. It literally feels as if the spine is on fire.

Treat it with the utmost respect and caution, and allow this force to operate like everything else in nature – *slowly*.

Levitation

When something rises in the air, either a body or an object, it is a form of psychokinesis, reversing gravity. Bodily levitation was first recorded centuries before Christ and is still supposed to take place among Buddhist monks today, not so much for curiosity as for necessity in the moment. Often, getting from place to place meant crossing deep rivers and the only way across would be to levitate. Records of levitation in the lives of the saints number more than 200 and often such people are said to have risen in the air while praying or in a state of meditation or rapture. This was interpreted as a sign of God's favour and the raising of the heart and mind to him.

How is it done? I have never had a direct experience but the yogis claim that certain breathing techniques practised over long periods of time can make the body as light as a feather by decreasing specific gravity enough for the body to float in the air or travel in the sky at thousands of miles a minute. Others say that it is a state of mind and consciousness. Those who practise transcendental meditation and breathing techniques have achieved a sort of frog hop, raising themselves some eighteen inches off the ground. But what is it all for?

The raising of objects has been recorded many times but probably the most dramatic is at a temple in India near Puna, which is dedicated to the Sufi saint, Qmar Ali Dervish. Outside the mosque is a boulder weighing 120 lb. It only takes seven or more pilgrims to touch it with their index fingers and chant 'Qmar Ali Dervish', and the boulder obligingly rises some six feet into the air, staying there for a few seconds before coming down again. Again, I would question, what is the point of it all? Perhaps you have the answer?

Ley Lines

Ley lines were rediscovered in this century in 1921 by Alfred Watkins. The word 'ley' is an old Saxon word meaning alignment or land temporarily under grass. Watkins called his alignment, straight tracks, and found that they usually passed through ancient monuments, medieval buildings, churches, castles and manor houses. It has been established that a ley crosses England from Tintagel in Cornwall through the stone circle of Avebury to St Albans and beyond while another extends from St Albans Head in Dorset, again through Avebury and up as far as Lindisfarne off the Northumbrian coast. These lines are described by Dion Fortune, the occultist, in her books as 'lines of force between power centres'. Ancient sites of sun worship and power, our ancestors used them to contact the old pagan gods. It is possible to dowse for ley lines, but it is also possible to stand on them, sensing the electricity beneath your feet. Be careful if you dowse in stone circles, however, for many people report feelings of dizziness, sickness or disorientation. Energy can actually explode from the stones so treat it with the respect it deserves. Recent research on the Rollright Stones in Oxfordshire has shown that the earth energy flowing between sacred sites is not a myth. Scientists have proved several ley lines by fluctuations in a local magnetic field converging on the geomantric centre of the circle. Dowsers have also confirmed this and discovered that the magnetic pattern inside the circle of standing stones forms a seven-ring spiral. At long last scientists, using geiger counters, are doing what dowsers and sensitives have been doing for years.

Ley lines are lines of energy-flow along the surface of the earth, lines which are flows of natural earth energy, and are the way that the earth rebalances the energies of its physical body. There are similar lines of energy flowing in the human body and these are the lines called meridians, treated by the Chinese art of acupuncture or acupressure. Some researchers believe that, if the various power centres of each country were linked up, they would form a planetary grid covering the whole earth. Stalactite photographs have revealed recently that our planet really does project ridges and geo-physical features to form a regulated grid. This consists of twelve pentagon-shaped sections superimposed over a system of twenty equilateral triangles. It has also been shown that hurricanes blow up at the points where the network crosses and that ocean currents and winds follow its outlines. It is also thought that the weak points in the planetary grid are the areas such as the Devil's Sea near Japan and the Bermuda Triangle. These areas could be gateways to other dimensions and certainly experience freak weather and atmospheric effects not felt elsewhere.

Many great ley lines in Britain are found through power centres and sacred sites of pre-Christian era. Dowsers often find that these sites are situated above underground springs and streams. In China, ley lines are called Dragon Paths or Feng Shui, and local dowsers are in great demand to offer advice on the best place to build a new house, to be buried or to site a temple, so that its position will harmonize with the flow of energy from the earth. Often, leys have a very deep religious meaning as well, as they were used as pilgrims' routes between sacred places.

How do you know if you are on a ley? If you stand in front of the altar in any great cathedral you are probably standing on a ley line. Our ancestors didn't just build anywhere! Walk up and down the nave of the cathedral, being very conscious of a feeling through your feet like a tingling or slight electric current. You can also feel this very strongly in places like Glastonbury Abbey, Stonehenge and Avebury as several ley lines converge on

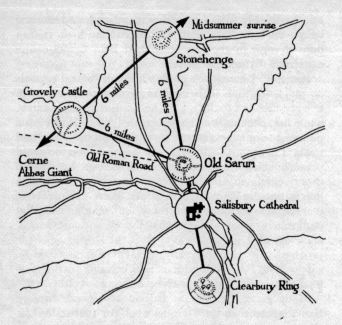

these great ruins. With practise you will know when your feet are on the ley line or not. An alternative method is to use a pendulum and just simply dowse for the line. It is not only in the past that our ancestors knew where to build on major power-points, for today's spiritual communities have also been guided to do just that. The Findhorn Community in Forres, Scotland was guided to build their temple where five ley lines intersect and the White Eagle Lodge in Liss, Hampshire is the site of six ley line intersections. In Glastonbury two major ley lines intersect in my aunt's house! I hasten to add that her house is the other side of the Glastonbury Abbey wall.

What do you do when you find a ley line? As ley lines can run the length and breadth of Britain and beyond to other countries, you can put a great deal of energy into them which has far-reaching effects. Standing on a ley line, preferably with a crystal in your hand, and sending your own love, light and positive energy down it, can only strengthen the line itself and help disperse any negativity that may be there.

Recently, I have been guided to plant several crystals on major ley lines in Britain and America. In America one crystal went to the top of the Empire State Building, while another one was buried in the White House on a powerful ley line which ran right through its centre and straight on through Congress and beyond. You too could plant crystals where you feel there is negative energy, programming them to absorb the energy and transform it into positive energy. Believe me, there are plenty of places where ley lines meet, wherever you may live, that need this.

Do try it.

Love

You were born to learn about love. For that indeed, is the lesson of planet earth. Love is power and how you tap into that power and use it depends on your individual consciousness. It is possible to have affection and it is possible to have really great love for love is an act of being and its beauty encompasses everything.

Do you love yourself? This is where it all starts, for without that self-love, that nourishment, you cannot love other people. To love yourself, you need to have a measure of self-esteem and then, and only then, can you develop intimacy with someone else. Love is often defined as affectionate devotion and parental benevolence but it is this and much, much more. It is worth taking a good look at yourself to see how you love. In close relationships, can you really be yourself and still appreciate your partner? Being possessive, jealous or trying to keep control of the situation is not loving. Fearing intimacy and keeping yourself closed down and secretive is not loving. Refusing to share on all levels is not loving. Being able to love wholeheartedly is being able to be yourself and to share yourself and to appreciate, care and nurture those around you. Loving is being able to give without thought of return and to create an atmosphere of harmony and joy.

Love is the most basic essential for living. A new-born baby can die if there is no love. Many people today are being kept alive medically by the wonders of science but are they really alive if they are not loving human beings? And loved? Bring more love to yourself and you'll bring more into your environment and into your life. Remember the words of John the Apostle.

'Beloved, let us love one another: for love is of God;
and everyone that loveth is born of God, and knoweth God.
He that loveth not knoweth not God; for God is love.'

I John 4: 7-8

Lucifer

How art thou fallen from heaven, O Lucifer, son of the morning!

Isaiah 14:12

Lucifer, meaning 'light bearer', is the name that the Romans gave to the morning star. The only reason that Lucifer is associated with Satan and the Devil image is because he was an archangel who tried to make himself the equal of God; consequently, he became the scapegoat of all that is seen as bad. Lucifer has been used by sorcerers and the black arts, for it said that he is the chief of devils and the Lord of Darkness. They often make pacts with him, submitting to his will and their own lust and perversions. The Christian Church has developed a ridiculous image of Lucifer, blaming him for everything that the Church felt was of pagan nature, but Lucifer can only reflect what is already inside the self. If you want to get into a frenzy and tap into some pretty grim energies, then that is your responsibility and nobody else's. All Lucifer does is reflect the ignorance and self-indulgence of the parts of your own nature that you have not yet controlled or understood. Lucifer did challenge the hierarchy and lost, but it is also stated that Lucifer will one day return, and then the most beautiful angel that ever existed will take his rightful place beside the Creator. The whole manifestation of the Lucifer idea comes down to the fact that, within us all, we have that Luciferan aspect in our personality, and it is through our own determination and effort that we can raise ourselves above this aspect and reach our real self.

Macrocosm and Microcosm

The macrocosm is like a giant oak tree that has been growing longer than anyone can remember. Its trunk is large and its branches stretch far and wide. This monumental tree has born witness to many things during its life. The microcosm is like the seed of the tree, the acorn which falls to the ground or is taken by a bird or animal and lost in the foliage. Other acorns get carried great distances before they take root. But, gradually, the acorn grows into a tree. It's a different tree in a different location but it has the same quality and strength as its creator, the giant oak tree. It has its own struggles and is left completely on its own but, when it does grow up, it has within it all the qualities and strengths of its parent. It has also gained a new experience. It, too, drops acorns and when it is time for the giant oak tree to retract into the ground one of its acorns may well be on the way towards growing into a giant.

The macrocosm is all the universe, galaxies, solar system and all the space in between; we call this God.

The microcosm is a smaller version and is the cells, molecules, atoms, sub-atomic particles and all the space in between them; the particular form that this takes is man. The universe, therefore, is regarded as a human organism on a colossal scale, and man is a miniature copy, just like the giant oak tree and the acorn. The same idea follows through because man, who is created in the image of God, is destined to gain enough knowledge, wisdom and understanding to grow from his acorn state into a giant tree. The words, 'as above, so below', reflect the idea that man is a perfect replica of the macrocosm and that his divine gifts can help him raise his consciousness to such an extent that he will go beyond time and space and grow big enough to encompass all the physical and spiritual realms. It may seem incredible that man is capable of such great things but, just as we can see the potential in the acorn, so our hearts and minds can grow large enough to comprehend the cosmic scale. The universe used to be an immense ball of life-essence that was in total harmony and oneness with itself. This was in its passive state, but the forces of change gradually built up to such a point that the life-essence had to move. The explosion sent pockets of life-force flying across the universe. One of these pockets was mankind; it still vibrated at the same rate as the harmonious ball of life but it experienced separateness, just as did the acorn when it fell off the tree. This pocket of essence divided again and again until there were millions of fragments and some of them formed into individual spirits which gradually experienced more intense form of separateness by entering into dense, physical matter. Each unit still had a small fragment deep inside itself that vibrated at the same rate as the life-essence that penetrates every living thing, the same vibration as God. The idea is that, when the universal essence has been in its creative state long enough, expanding in size and consciousness, it will gradually start to contract over millions of years and all those fragments will come together again. This will not be in the same way as before, because some have grown into large oak trees and so the giant oak tree will, over millions of years, have grown a few more branches.

Magic

The word 'magic' conjures up more things in people's minds than anything else, and it is hard to distinguish what is magic and what is not. Magic is a form of manipulation for 99.9 per cent of the people who use it and is a manipulation of the energies around them, usually for their own selfish or possessive needs. For the remaining 0.1 per cent, magic is a total devotion and tuning in to natural forces. Part of your purpose on earth is to integrate spirit with matter and, by doing this, you really fulfil your destiny. You are a spiritual being in a dense physical body and need to spread light and intensity of spirit into physical matter.

You not only have to understand how these things work but you must literally open yourself to let the spirit in. By doing this, you raise the physical atoms and molecular structures of your body to a higher and higher vibration. To be able to do this, you need to study physical energies and understand what they do and do not do. This is the very basis of all investigations, scientifically and mystically. People who are spiritually evolved are able to understand what this means, and these people are magicians. They are able to use natural forces in a balanced way, allowing the spirit to enter into dense physical matter.

The study of magic has led to a great deal of abuse and most magic is concerned with manipulation and a denial of the original concept. This can mean, however, that more can be learnt although it takes a fine mind and a fine heart and a fine spirit to even begin to use the real forces of magic. These magical forces are not white or black, they just are. They are the natural processes of spirit being able to enter into dense, physical matter and there are certain methods, certain ceremonies and certain initiations that a spiritual being can do, to allow spirit to enter into matter. A magician who is well versed in universal magic is the only person who is capable of doing this and, during our whole time on planet earth, there have never been more than one hundred people who can be called magicians. Others are struggling towards the central goal and still others are not even aware of it.

Overall, the whole scene of magic looks like a vast, black cloud, and only at the centre is there a very small light. But that small light is more brilliant than the whole of that black cloud and, as soon as we start to understand what magic is really about, the larger that light will become. When this happens it will eventually disperse the cloud in a fraction of a second. But that is not the way of things and we have to wait for all the people that created that cloud to find their light, and therefore disperse and transmute their own energy.

Magic Chants

Abracadabra is one example that people know and it has been said that Merlin first uttered this magic word. Originally it dates from the time of the Norman conquerors, and was often found on a piece of parchment and was hung around the necks of the Norman soldiers, as they believed it would protect them and bring them victory. It is, in fact, the triangle formed by the word that contains the magic.

Magicians

The knowledge and teachings of magic are known as the occult, meaning hidden or secret. The hidden teachings are the science of the ancient philosophers, called magi, a word which stems from magus, meaning priest, wise and excellent. The most famous among the magi were the three kings who came to worship Jesus in Bethlehem. Moses, Solomon, Merlin, Hermes Trismagistus, Albertus, Magnus, Alastair Crowley, Madame Blavatsky, are some of the people who practised as magicians; each of them had a colourful and astounding life. Merlin, for example, is reputed to have been a member of the Druids and believed to be responsible for the birth and enthronement of King Arthur. The legend tells of a crystal cave where he lived and worked, having the ability to speak with gods and animals. One of the things that he was held responsible for was the transportation of the entire group of giant stones to Stonehenge, which he is supposed to have brought across the sea from Ireland by teleportation.

Usually, the magician either works on his own or joins one of the secret orders. The last famous order on record was the Order of the Golden Dawn, founded in London by three masons in 1877. This revived a serious study and practice of magic, changing the image of magic from theatrics to recognizing real forces of nature. Some of its members were Alastair Crowley, W.B. Yeats and Dion Fortune. Crowley eventually broke with the Golden Dawn and founded his own order called the Silver Star. His magical system, which he called magick, has been described as a house within a house, and is probably the most monumental contribution to occultism since the Middle Ages. His exploits as a poet, writer, painter, master chess player, mountaineer, devoted lecher, drug addict and master magician, took Victorian England by storm, and his showmanship and brilliance continued right up to his death in 1947.

The driving force behind a magician is not so much to dominate others as to strengthen his own personality and inner self so that he can bring some sort of control over his environment and life in general. Magic is simply the conscious or unconscious application of the laws of nature through the power of will. We all use the power of will at different times and in different degrees. Sometimes we use will by consciously drawing on it all the time and getting distraught or disillusioned if the desired effect does not come about. The difference between a magician and the average person is that the magician is conscious of channelling his will to bring about the desired result. Most of us who may want something consciously tend to dissipate the power of our will because things do not occur as quickly or as slowly as we want them to, or the thing we are after is beyond our sphere of availability.

The magician, if he is trained properly and understands his own art, will know what is possible and what is not at any particular time. Anything outside his sphere can only come to him by increasing his power and understanding or by realizing what he has got and using it properly. A magician sees that there are no impossibilities, only probabilities, so what he does is to widen his sphere of availability so that there are more probable things within his grasp. With knowledge, understanding and discipline at his disposal, the magician can accomplish many things usually denied to the average person. What you normally hear about is the magician who has tried to obtain things outside his availability, using manipulation and force. This is due to lack of understanding of what his art is all about. There have been many cases of this, usually sensational cases, which is why we tend to hear about them as distinct from serious magic. A magician needs positive thoughts and feelings and confidence in himself and his abilities, but greed and envy will always, as with anything else, turn everything sour.

The forces involved in magical practices are the same that you and I use in our everyday life. When you are positive and channel your energies into something, it is quite amazing what you can achieve. When you recognize your sphere of availability and enjoy what you have, instead of grasping at everything else, then you have conquered and understood something of a very profound nature. You don't have to join a group to be a magician. You only have to be yourself; recognize your own strength and weaknesses; always give of your best; be patient; recognize your limitations, but always keep your mind and heart open so you can expand who and what you are; recognize and take up opportunities and, most important, have confidence in who and what you are.

Life is the best teacher. Whatever path you take will offer all the conditions to learn and expand your consciousness. Become aware of the fact that magic is part of the struggle by human beings to control their environment as well as their inner self. If you consider yourself a person who is struggling to keep your life together, then you can perhaps qualify to become a magician.

Mandala

It is possible to find mandalas in many places today, but it hasn't always been that way. A mandala is usually a very complex design, a mystical symbol of immensely concentrated quality and it is always a circle enclosing a square. The circle is a magical one and is composed of a variety of symbols. A mandala tends to be abstract in design. Buddists and Hindus use mandalas a good deal, especially for meditation, and they believe that, if you meditate properly, you will first perceive the mandala as a map of the world and then see it as yourself, and finally you indentify yourself with the cosmos. Rather like a mantra, its main use is for meditation and, by focusing on such a complex wheel or square, the outer mind is kept fully occupied while the inner attention can be used with greater concentration. My husband and I were recently given a gift of a mandala each which a friend had been inspired to paint. The colours as well as the design are extremely significant and the meaning of each part needs to be considered with great care. As a meditation symbol they are certainly worth experimenting with. Kay who painted ours, found that each one, as she worked, was a meditation in itself.

Mantra

A mantra is a hymn of praise and, by the power of its cosmic vibration, can create changes. The Om is the best-known mantra sound but the Om Mani Padmi Om is the name of the supreme deity of the Golden Lotus of Wisdom in Hindu religion, and is one of the most popular and powerful mantras. Mantras are used in meditation throughout the western world and work in meditation because sound drops below its own level. If you say your mantra over and over again in your mind as a meditation, the sound has to drop from the conscious mind to the subconsious. Saying a mantra is a form of conscious auto-suggestion, a means of reaching the subconscious mind through constant repetition. Psychological research has shown that such a method can only become truly effective if the sound is meaningless. This is the key to bypass the barrier between the conscious and unconscious minds. In a sense the mantra is a way of tricking the conscious mind in order to reach the realms of the subconscious that lie beyond.

The eastern writer, Wei Wo Wei, said, 'A mantra is not intended to be subjected to conceptual interpretation, therefore it need not be given a literal translation. It is an esoteric medium for the appreciation of what universally is.'

Sometimes the mantra can drop as low as the spiritual

self and then you experience true bliss. Most of the time, however, it drops into the subconscious and does an awful lot of good by bringing up old fears, guilt feelings, and belief systems. I teach a mantra meditation as well as using one myself.

Materialization

A popular form of materialization in the early 1900s was the manufacture of ectoplasm from different parts of the body. It was thought that the medium would allow entities and spirits to come through the body so that they could manifest in varying degrees of solidification. Ectoplasm is cold to the touch, slightly luminous and has a smell reminiscent of ozone. It varies in colour from pure white to black. If it is touched unexpectedly or a light is turned on during the manifestation, it will immediately fly back into the medium causing pain and bruising to the medium's body. It usually manifests very slowly, first as a vapour that gradually turns into a semi-fluid consistency; but it has been known to go as solid as a rod of iron. Gradually, the face or a form of the spirit will become clearer and there are several photographs and well-documented cases of such happenings although it is becoming an exceedingly rare phenomenon today.

There was considerable argument at the turn of the century as to whether ectoplasm ever existed. The only specimen turned out to consist of several manmade constituents such as egg white and cheese cloth.

The most famous case of materialization was that of Madame Elizabeth d'Esperance. In the early 1900s she did many materialization displays of a young Arab girl called Yolande. Several times during the materialization, Yolande was seized by some sitters but, when the light was put on, they only found that they were holding on to the medium. Elizabeth was ill every time this happened and once a sitter tried to violate the phantom girl. The medium's hair suddenly turned white and she was confined to her bed for two years. The strangest incident then occurred as the medium's body underwent a partial dematerialization. On one occasion her body from the waist down completely disappeared, this being vouched for by responsible witnesses.

Another form of materialization is known as 'apports'. In this situation the object will suddenly disappear, be transported to another location and then reappear. The occurrence of this is based on the idea that, by use of will power, matter can be taken apart, transported to another place, and then put back together without changing its form. This is achieved by the mind of a person who concentrates and controls the whole process. The theory suggests that there is an unknown form of matter beyond the solid, liquid, and gaseous state – a fluid state which is invisible to the naked eye. When matter is in this state, it can be willed to travel at the speed of thought, moving through any physical barriers such as walls or even solid steel. It has been noticed that stone or metallic objects are often hot when they arrive at their destination; this suggests that some change has occurred in their molecular vibration. Another theory assumes that objects enter into the fourth dimension, a higher frequency of space and time. The objects are believed to be lifted into this fourth dimension, taken to their destination, and then dropped back into three-dimensional space. This process can be reversed and the object can disappear from one space and appear in another space; this is still known as apport. A considerable variety of objects have been known to be apported; they range from a glassful of wine, a plant over five feet high, and an ape-like creature. It has been proved that mind can affect matter, but whether it can do it to the extent of making objects disappear and reappear is up to the individual to decide.

Meditation

Meditation is a discipline which enables the individual to get in touch with the inner self. In order to do this you need to train the mind, either by the use of a mantra or a thought or symbol. If you think of the mind like a busy telephone switchboard, the first three lines are taken up with the humdrum details of daily life, but the last three lines are the real inner self. In order to gain access to line four, you need to keep the first three lines engaged and busy, and this is really what meditation is all about.

The mind in its undisciplined state is constantly active but its activity is largely aimless and unproductive with little sustained attention or concentration. We think all the time of trivial events, idle fantansies or worries which fritter away the energies of the mind. To meditate is to establish yourself in charge of this powerhouse of thought and to bring the mind into obedience to the will. This is not done overnight! Control of the mind is acquired gradually by regular practice over a period of time. The first thing is to be physically still and comfortable. Try to be as relaxed as possible and mentally work from the toes to the head, making sure there is no tension or stress in the body. Talk to your body. Ask the muscles to relax and let go. Don't try to sit in a yoga position if this is not for you but put cushions on the floor or put a cushion on a chair and get yourself really comfortable. Take your shoes off. Make sure the lighting is not too harsh; it is much easier to relax with very little light, such as candlelight.

Everyone can learn to meditate as it is so very simple, but it takes an initiate to know which meditation would suit you best. If you decide on a mantra meditation, you simply allow yourself to choose a mantra which appeals to you and there are many thousands of words which have no meaning but are just simply sounds. Having chosen one, then do stick to it for at least a year and don't change if nothing happens. It is the continuous repetition of the mantra that works the magic. Sit quietly and take the phone off the hook and kick your shoes off, making sure that no one disturbs you for at least twenty minutes. Do put pets out of the room as well; they enjoy the energy that you achieve through meditation which won't leave you a lot as a result! Close your eyes and simply observe your breath and the way that the chest rises and falls. Start the mantra, almost at the back of your mind, and do it silently and allow yourself to relax. Thoughts and feelings are bound to come up and, when they do, go back to the mantra and to the breathing. You are not meant to think of nothing or to do nothing, it simply is not the way this happens. Other meditations I teach connect the individual with the spirit guide and this meditation is, in fact, a communication. In the past, yogis, ascetics and spiritualist groups seemed to use meditation exclusively, but now it is open to anyone, mostly because of the immense popularity of transcendental meditation and Zen Buddhism. Whether you use meditation to relax or to achieve cosmic and spiritual insight really doesn't matter. In our tension-laden world, we need time to be quiet and to allow ourselves personal space. Meditation is the only way I know.

Miracles

To me every hour of the light and dark is a miracle,
Every cubic inch of space is a miracle.

Walt Whitman
'Miracles' in *Leaves of Grass*

Miracles are an example of a flow of energy taking its natural form without any hindrance from man. When a natural miracle takes place, it is only the order of things coming together quite naturally, the natural cycle. Whether our minds are able to accept that, or do not see that there is a natural order of things, is neither here nor there.

Miracles that are often talked about are the ones that were done by the Master Jesus, such as turning water into wine or feeding the five thousand or walking on water. If you go into these, you will find that many other events took place around the miracles that assisted in these things happening in their natural order. Some of them didn't actually physically happen, but there is a message, and a special energy in portraying these things in the form of a story. For many people the *idea* of a miracle makes things seem special. There are miracles in your everyday life: when somebody is born, when somebody recovers from a great illness, when somebody falls in love and finds that special something in another person. These are all miracles and very natural ones. Every year in the spring, another miracle takes place, the rebirth of a natural cycle of prosperity and growth.

Perhaps the greatest miracle story of all is one that my husband told me. He was guided to go from London to Mount Shasta in California to await a miracle. He earnestly believed on his journey over there and up the difficult mountainside that he would be shown some door into the mountain where tremendous knowledge had been stored throughout the ages. He was guided to sleep on the mountain and was awakened early next morning and told to stand on a particular rock right near the summit. At that moment the sun rose. In his heart he knew that this was the miracle he had come so far to see. It is one that we can all see every day, but how few of us stand and wonder at such a sight?

Look all around you and you'll find there are miracles in everything that occurs. Our physical body is a miracle, and all of natural life is a miracle. When you look at it in this way, you see that it is only natural for certain things to happen. Things that years ago would have been considered a miracle are very normal for us today. Flying around the world, travelling at great speeds, seeing pictures from the other side of the world instantaneously could be considered miracles, depending on your point of view.

The most profound miracle that can take place is if you find your true self, something beyond your normal behaviour, beyond the normal intellect, beyond your fears. Inside of you is a miracle and outside is a miracle. Everything is a miracle and, if you can allow the miracle outside to flow through you, and the miracles inside you to flow out, then you will find that all the miracles will merge together as one, and that truly will be a miracle.

Music and Sound

Seated one day at the organ,
I was weary and ill at ease,
And my fingers wandered idly
Over the noisy keys.

I do not know what I was playing,
Or what I was dreaming then;
But I struck one chord of music,
Like a sound of a great Amen.

Adelaide Anne Procter
'A Lost Chord'

The world that I live in and you live in is alive with sound and sound has a tremendous effect not only on our physical but also on our psychological and spiritual state of being. This has always been the way throughout time.

The human body can be taught to be very harmonious with the use of music and sound, or can be made stressful, tense and disjointed. During ancient initiation rites in Egypt and Atlantis, music was an important part of the preparation. Whether it was harps, lyres, flutes, trumpets, cymbals or drums, the initiate could be put into trance through the appropriate melodies. This didn't only happen in Egypt, for it also occurred in Tibet, Greece and in the Americas.

Certain people, such as Dennis Stoll, the late Sir Thomas Beecham's deputy, have the clairaudiant ability to be inside a pyramid or temple in Egypt today and to hear the sounds as they were played in ancient times. Pythagoras, who had definite views on musical philosophy, taught that the lyre, as well as all other music of the time, was the creation of the gods. The music played by our ancestors didn't jangle the nerves but created a sense of harmony and well-being. Chanting and bell ringing create a wonderful feeling of joy.

Experiment a little yourself and you will see certain types of rock and roll or punk music make you feel really agitated and nervous while some classical or harmonious tunes produce a relaxing, possibly drowsy, effect. I very much doubt, whether in the past, the volume of sound was as great as it is today for often musicians with little training tend to compensate with a great sound rather than great expertise. Most of the instruments used in the past could create and echo and it is only recently, in modern-day music, that this same echo is found. It suggests a bouncing of sound off many distant surfaces and, for me at least, brings back strong memories of initiation rites in the past. If plants respond so dramatically to sound that is harmonious, just consider what disharmonious sound is doing to your own body. If you want to develop your ESP and psychic ability, surround yourself with mellow and comforting sound. Music that inspires and uplifts will nourish you far more than music and sound that produce discord, tension and shattered nerves.

Many people feel tremendously comforted by listening to music such as Gregorian chants, but perhaps the most uplifting of all is the wonderful sound of the Om. When the Om or Aum is sounded by a group in unison it is the most beautiful experience. This mystical holy word really does precede all prayers.

Names

Throughout the world and throughout history, names and naming have been of great importance in religion, magic, the occult, psychic phenomena and mythology. In ancient Egypt not to have a name was a terrible curse. It was the worst possible thing that could happen to you. The Egyptians believed that not to have a name meant that, when you died, you couldn't go on but would fall backwards into the void. Criminals had their name taken away when charged with their crime; it was simply as if they didn't exist. It was worse even than disgrace for it meant there was no hope for eternity. Moyra, a friend of mine, remembers a life she had as a temple oracle in the time of Aknatnan when she was kept on drugs in order to perform in the temple. To make her anonymous she had no name and she remembers vividly the heartache it caused and the feeling of not being a person.

A name can indeed be independent of the object with which it is identified and could give someone power over the person or the object. If you change your name, then you certainly change your vibration. Several years ago, I changed my name from Ann to Tara, and my whole personality changed at the same time. It has taken quite a long time for my mother to call me Tara, but eventually she has succeeded and now nearly everyone accepts it. Certain religions often give a change of name on joining them and it is quite common to have a spiritual name as well as a given one. It wasn't only in primitive times that names were often secret to prevent their use by enemies. If you were born in China, then your name was only ever revealed to the local astrologer or priest, and you had another name for daily use. Also the name of Jewish 'Yahweh' is only sounded once a year by the rabbi of the synagogue in the Holy of Holies.

If someone knows your name they know your vibration. When you develop enough to contact your spirit guide, you link into them by repeating the name three times. This rarely fails. It is very important that you are happy with your own name. Unfortunately, most of us have parents who aren't tuned into such things and who give us names because they are fashionable or simply because they liked someone of that name at sometime or another. I was named Margaret Ann at the time that everyone was naming their children after the Royal princesses. I was never called Margaret as it was considered too long, and my parents had to resort to Ann for many years.

It is important if you are expecting a baby or know someone who is, to ask the mother to tune in to the soul of the child and to be sensitive enough to find the right name. When I was expecting my son John I knew he would be a boy and I had various names in mind, such as Timothy and Andrew. While I was in labour I read a magazine feature about a little boy called Jonathon and, although the name Jonathon had never come up in my life before, I knew that this was his name. It was almost as if someone had given me the magazine deliberately and made sure that I read it. Perhaps they had? When Jonathon was twelve years old, he announced he was changing his name. He is now called John and is very happy with it and, indeed, this is his spiritual name. If you are not happy with the name your parents gave you do meditate upon it and think about it at great length and see if another one comes into your mind. Not because it is fashionable and not because it is the name of a filmstar or pop singer, but just because you resonate to the sound and feel very, very comfortable with it.

Nightmares

Nightmares are dreams of a frightening or horrific nature that mostly cause an abrupt awakening and terror in the heart.

We believe that, if we put a sheet over our heads, the monster will go away. Why the monster has bothered to come to us and why a thin sheet is capable of making the monster disapper does not really matter. Since medieval times, monsters were believed to come in the form of a demon called incubus, that raped women during the night. It was reported that there was a heavy pressure on the chest and a feeling also of being smothered. A monster-thought represents a fear within our minds, which could be caused by something that we have seen, heard or done, that cannot be revealed or resolved, and so we block it within ourselves. The only way that it can be released is when the conscious mind is in a state of relaxation and this occurs in the dream state.

There are also exterior forces involved in some nightmares, because, when you're in a nervous or distraught condition, your sleeping pattern is disturbed and lack of sleep makes you vulnerable and weak. Everybody who consciously projects across the regions of the mind, and many do, takes advantage of your fears and weaknesses, causing your sleep to be disturbed and conjuring up everything nasty that you fear. Most of the time, though, it is your own mind that creates the nightmare and sometimes the cause of the nightmares goes back years and years to childhood. If you suppress something inside you it will, eventually, have to come out and one of the ways is through a nightmare. Alternatively, you could become ill or have an accident, or maybe even a mental disorder. The nightmare is the bogeyman inside of you and, if you suffer with this, it would be wise to seek counselling or help from somebody who understands these things.

Numerology

Numerology is the art of predicting by numbers and can provide an extremely interesting and accurate insight into character and personality. It requires no extra-sensory powers, but it is simply worked out mathematically. In its simplest form it is based upon the symbolic meanings and interpretations attached to the numbers 1 to 9. When you go for a reading, it is a good idea to jot down some of the major events of your life, such as when you went to school or university, when you got married, when your children were born, etc., thus enabling you to confirm the dates that come up with the numerologist. The reader needs your full name together with the date of birth. As the date of birth is already in numbers, that is very straightforward, but the name requires that letters be converted into numbers; this is usually done using the following table:

1	2	3	4	5	6	7	8	9
A	B	C	D	E	F	G	H	I
J	K	L	M	N	O	P	Q	R
A	T	U	V	W	X	Y	Z	

For example:

L O N D O N
3 6 5 4 6 5 = 29 = 11 = 2

Each letter is converted into a digit and the name is processed by totalling and progressively reducing the totals until a simple digit total is achieved for the whole name. One thing that will not work is giving a false date of birth because you will certainly be shown up immediately! The name is also important, so give the name that you are known by and not the name with which you were christened.

Numerology shows that your life runs in cycles, that is, fourteen, seven, three years, etc. It is a fascinating art and it should not be forgotten that Pythagoras considered numbers the secret of the universe and that, throughout history, they have been given magical, mystical powers. For the Greeks, three, the essence of the triangle, was all-important. Tradition has it that odd numbers are masculine and even numbers are feminine. Seven has always been a magic number and, although many people believe thirteen to be unlucky, others consider it to be the luckiest of all.

Pythagoras, 500 BC, taught that the world is built upon the power of numbers. Any modern-day gypsy would probably tell you the same! Pythagoras, however, maintained that the numbers from 1-9 were the universal primaries and each had a specific significance:

1. Aggression, ambition and action; also the number of the tyrant.

2. The number of balance and contrast; opposites, polarities, antithesis, also of equilibrium and harmony. It is the number of male and female.

3. Represents time and fate, the past, the present and the future. It is the number of the family, father, mother and child and also variability, adaptability and change. It shows a happy and talented person.

4. This is the foundation number and represents the points of the compass, the elements of earth, air, fire and water and the seasons. It is called the primitive number.

5. Is the number of chance and links the opposites. Good for adventurers, new experiences and the fearless.

6. This is the number of perfection, being divisible by two and three, and represents harmony, beauty and trust.

7. The magical number represents mysteries, the occult, clairvoyance and magic. It also represents the seven principles in man, the universe, as well as the seven planets, the days of the week and the notes on a musical scale.

8. This is the number of materialism and represents all that is solid and complete. When halved its parts are equal. It is the number of balance.

9. The greatest of all primary numbers signifies hope and achievement and contains the qualities of all the others. Three times three is most propitious. A magician is said to control the forces of nature through this number.

How can you use numbers in day-to-day life? If you find out your lucky number you will soon find out which days are lucky and most propitious for you. Use your birth and name numbers and add these to the date of the day and see what comes up. The study of numbers alone is more of a game than anything else but, with clairvoyant ability, some very striking results can be achieved.

Obsession

To be obsessed is to be in a state where the mind, emotions and spirit are influenced by a negative force such as a demon, devil or ghost which makes the individual act out of character. It can achieve complete possession if it goes on long enough. Usually a ghost or disincarnate spirit will be attracted by their own obsession so, if you start taking drugs or becoming a heavy drinker, someone with that type of craving from the low astral levels might seek you out and attach himself to you. I have exorcized several people to whom this has happened. Too much of anything does not help the developing psychic! Jesus could cast out evil spirits, devils or demons, and so can many people today although it is much better not to attract them in the first place and saves an awful lot of bother.

Omens

Lamentings heard i' the air; strange screams of death,
And prophesying with accents terrible
Of dire combustion and confused events
New hatch'd to be the woeful time. The obscure bird
Clamour'd the livelong night: some say, the earth
Was feverous and did shake.

William Shakespeare
Macbeth, Act II, Scene iii

When a black cat runs in front of you, it immediately
conjures up the idea that something good is about to
happen. There are hundreds of small incidences in your
everyday life, and yet some things seem to warn you
either of danger or that good fortune is close. By
recognizing and responding to omens, you can avoid
misfortune or put all your energy and effort into
something by knowing that you're on the right track.
The sky has always been a good source of omens and the
rainbow must be the favourite, for it always means good
fortune and happiness. A shooting star is also seen as a
good omen, while an eclipse is considered a bad omen,
telling of future disaster or bad weather during the year.
At home a falling picture, or the stopping of the tick of a
clock, means a death in the family, while dreaming of
death is an omen of birth. Finding nine perfect peas in a
pod is a fruitful marriage, and a swarm of bees is a sign of
future prosperity.

Omens are a catalogue of changes in our normal
environment that reflect what is going on inside of
ourselves. Real omens do seem to make a distinct
impression on our minds, whether they come while we
are awake or asleep. Some omens are a result of the
unconscious mind going forward and checking something out, and revealing it to the conscious mind through
omens. Sometimes omens are for a whole country or even
the whole world, and these occur when a comet or

148

unusual star can be seen. Nature does seem to reflect patterns of the future and the more sensitive you can become to real omens the more you understand what is around you and why it is there.

Oracles

The idea of an oracle has come about because it has always been a basic human need to know the future. The oracle is the revelation or inspiration from a divine source that is conveyed through a priest or priestess or, in modern terms, a medium. The belief is that, although consciously you cannot see the future, you may, when asleep or in some other altered state of consciousness, be capable of knowing events of the future. The most well-known oracle is the one at Delphi. Here the priestess went into a trance and Apollo was said to have talked through her, giving answers and advice. Most of the time, though, the answers were not very clear, and had to be translated by the priests; this led to a great deal of misinterpretation.

There are many forms of oracle like the *I Ching*, tarot or direct channelling through a medium. The medium or the cards, are used as a vehicle to reflect what is inside you, giving a synopsis of how the situation occurred, what the present situation is, and what you have to do to change the situation for the better. The skill of the person giving the session depends on his being able to reflect the situation as it is, rather than allowing his own ego and attitudes to affect it. The advice, whether it has come through your guide, his guide, his higher self or your higher self, has to be translated or channelled through him because he is the contact, therefore, it will be affected by his understanding. Some people are capable of being a clear channel, but remember that they are also on the path of self-discovery and self-development, so they do not have all the answers.

The other aspect of the oracle is that you learn through truth and so, if you are told events of the future, it will not fall into place or mean anything to you until after it has occurred, unless you are prepared to work very hard to understand what has been said and to realize why the particular situation is occurring. You may be told that you are going to have an accident, a break with a person, be subject to adverse conditions, or go through long periods of feeling in a mess. The question you have to ask is 'why?' and 'How do I get out of it?' You are the only one who can decide that you want to bring a change about within yourself and within your life. If things do seem to be repeating themselves, an oracle will only be able to tell you that you are still in a mess, and it is only after you have decided that you want to change that the oracle may be able to advise you on what to do next. Oracles can only tell you that the basic pattern of that particular moment, and your free will, determination, and exterior forces will constantly change the way the situation appears to you. My advice is to develop your own intuition and sort it out yourself, and only use an oracle from time to time and not as a total support.

Ouija Board

In Victorian times, when spiritualism was a parlour game, the Ouija board was part of the sitting-room scene. In the last decade the revival of parlour games has brought the Ouija board back into popularity. Oui/Ja is the combination of 'yes' in both French and German and the board is covered with letters and numbers. A guided glass or pendulum spells out words and sentences from which information can be obtained. Unfortunately, very few valid, sensible messages ever come through Ouija boards and it can cause far more harm than good, unless there is a person with genuine psychic ability controlling it. Often the Ouija board is referred to as a planchette;

this is a slight improvement on the original board and is often used for automatic writing. With a planchette a heart-shaped piece of wood rests on small castors and is fitted with a pen pointing downwards which is guided by the user's hand. The messages that it creates on the paper underneath are due to the powers of the subconscious mind or a departed spirit. If the pen is not used then the board can be operated by two people putting their fingers on the heart-shaped piece of wood which will move along letters of the alphabet and numbers up to ten. Although this all started as a parlour game and as a harmless amusement, it can become a nightmare, especially if you decide to act upon a message from a source that you don't know and one that could be playing you like a fish on a hook.

This method is also similar to placing a wine glass in the centre of a Lexicon pack arranged in a circle on a table with a 'Yes' and 'No' card either side. By placing your finger on the glass it will move to indicate what is being communicated. The idea is again similar – that spirit communicators can spell out answers to questions.

All these methods can be extremely harmful and it should be remembered that the film 'The Exorcist' was based on a true story. This film has affected many people who, after seeing it, became agitated and some either committed suicide or were later placed in mental institutions. The true story was of a little boy, not a little girl, who played with a Ouija board and conjured up an evil spirit which gave him superhuman powers. The results were horrifying and caused several deaths. The fact that this is a *true* story says it all. So the answer is that, if you don't want to get more than you bargained for, don't play games with spirit communication. The trouble is that, with the Ouija board, the planchette or the finger-on-the-glass method, there is no control on who comes through. A trained medium has a 'doorkeeper' or control who allows spirit communicators access or *not*. The methods described here do not allow such control and therefore absolutely anything from the astral planes can take over. Not only the session but *YOU*! All Ouija boards should be banned and a law was recently passed in the UK to stop them being sold in children's toyshops as games. In my view, they should be banned altogether.

Out-of-Body-Experiences

Out-of-body experiences happen all the time but few people realize this or even understand what it is all about.

Not so long ago I was having lunch with a Fleet Street editor who was very worried indeed about experiences he was having at night. He was wondering who to consult in Harley Street to clear up the mystery. What he described to me happens to many, many people every single night, for he could see himself still on his bed but he could also see himself standing at the end of the bed looking back upon his body. This can, of course, be quite disconcerting if you don't understand what it is all about. Certainly I don't know anyone in Harley Street who could have given him the right explanation so his lunch with me was obviously fortuitous! An out-of-body experience doesn't necessarily have to happen at night for, although each of us experiences this nearly every night of our lives, we very seldom experience remembrance. It can happen any time during the day if we are in a daydreaming state or if we are sick or ill. The first time it happened to me I had been on a course of strong pain-killers after an accident and I suddenly realized that I could hear someone breathing heavily next to me in the bed (I have described this incident elsewhere). When I had the courage to open my eyes and see a wonderfully brilliant gold light centred on the 'I' part of myself, I was also aware of many people at the end of a golden tunnel and they were looking down at me as I was looking up at them. It was one of the highlights of my psychic development and a very joyful experience. Eventually I heard a noise and seemed to pop back into the physical body quite naturally without any strain or discomfort. It was such a good experience that I read everything I could on the subject but I have never exactly reproduced it in that particular way again.

Being out of the body is quite a normal and natural phenomenon and the fact that most of us don't remember what happens when we are asleep is a great pity. There is no doubt that people can remember a great deal and describe things that occur during the sleep state of which they could have had no prior knowledge. The most likely time that the experience will occur naturally is when you are near sleep and have a floating or flying sensation. If you can keep your mind from over-reacting and can go along with this floating feeling you could well drift easily out of the body and yet be conscious of the physical body at the same time. Alternatively, this experience can also be caused by illness. Many people, particularly if they have had an accident, will find themselves out of the body and looking back down on it. This is a very common occurrence indeed, for the minute the soul is threatened it will detach itself at the greatest possible speed! You'll be pleased to know, however, that there is a silver cord connecting the two bodies so unless the soul intends to leave the body permanently no harm can befall you whatsoever.

Astral projection, or out-of-body experience can open up a whole new world of the mind and provide plenty of new sensory experiences. Most people who experience this feel a rushing sound or a whirring sound in their heads, for in most recorded cases the astral body comes out through the head. It can also come out horizontally or be the result of a blackout. Often if we have woken suddenly from a particularly deep sleep we feel disorientated and not quite co-ordinated, and this is the result of our various bodies not being in line. The only way to correct this disorientation is to go back to sleep again immediately or to ask someone to make a very loud noise unexpectedly by your head. Projection can occur without being in the sleep state but this can only be done by an experienced sensitive although, on occasions, a very strong link like that between a mother and a child can produce this. I have in fact experienced this myself on more than one occasion. Perhaps the greatest lesson of out-of-body experiences is to reinforce the knowledge that life can exist outside the physical body; and that this is a perfectly natural experience for you, every day of your life – even if you don't remember it!

Palmistry

Most people have been asked at some time or other to cross a gypsy's palm with silver. Palmistry has been around for a long time, certainly since the time of Aristotle, 300 BC. Henry VIII forbade the study and practice by law but Queen Elizabeth I reinstated it, having such a regard for it that she created Dr John Dee her Royal Palmist and Astrologer. Palmists are quite numerous today. Probably the greatest of all was Cheiro, earlier this century. Remember, you can tell a great deal about someone by simply holding their hand. If the palms are thin and dry, they will tend to be nervous and unsure, but if they are thick and soft you can simply feel the sensuality! A firm palm shows energy while a flabby one tends to have a lazy owner. A hollow palm with very few mounts on it shows someone who is prone to ill health and negative thinking.

Everybody's palms are different and you will even find that your left hand is different from your right. A palmist looks at the lines on both hands and also the lines on your wrists and can work out your character and personality from the physical characteristics. Most people go to a palmist to find out about the future, but the past and present can also be seen. There are symbolic meanings attached to various lines and markings of the hands which can be interpreted. Most palmists I know simply use the hands as a crystal gazer uses a crystal ball. They simply need to tune into your vibration and, although they look at the lines the hands reveal, they are a point of focus for their clairvoyance far more than a scientific study. Other palmists use dividers and take exact measurements and are very mathematical indeed. Much research is being done on palmistry, and it has been found that certain markings on the skin of the hands do have medical significance and that there may be physical evidence underlying the practice of palmistry.

A serious palmist will begin by examining both hands. The left hand shows the potential with which you were born and the characteristics you inherited, while the right hand is thought to reflect how you have used that potential or how you may use it. It shows individuality and flexibility. If you are left-handed then reverse this out. To the palmist the first clue to your character and your destiny is the shape of your hands. If you have a square hand you are probably very practical, somewhat forceful and capable of achieving success. A conical hand, or a tapering hand, is likely to belong to a more artistic person, usually a communicator with great sensitivity. A hand shaped like a spade, which moves about a lot, shows someone with tremendous energy, full of positive action. The pointed hand is the hand of the idealist, often someone who is quite impractical and loves beauty and hates squalor. The long hand, which is often quite knotty at the joints, is the hand of the philosopher or thinker. You will probably find that your hand isn't exactly like one of these, but is a mixture of two or three. After the shape, the palmist will consider how flexible your hand is, for flexibility shows unconventionality; if there is great stiffness it will show stubbornness and determination to have your own way.

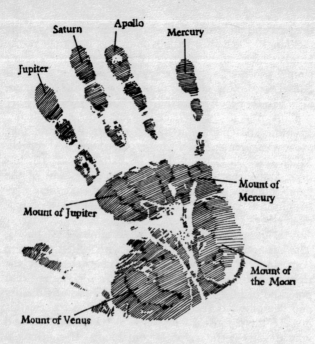

Stubborness is certainly shown in the angle of the thumb. A straight thumb shows less flexibility than one that shows quite a curve. If your thumb is set low at a wide angle to the hand it shows you could be careless whereas, if the thumb is set high on the hand, you are probably a more cautious, more inflexible character. Long fingers show a meticulous nature and a love of detail while short fingers usually show impatience and spontaneity. Check and see if the length of your second finger exceeds the distance from its knuckle to the wrist. This is considered long.

The lines on the hand can be extremely complex and criss-crossed or the main lines can be exceedingly simple like a clear map. The main lines are obvious: the heart line is the main line on the palm running from the second

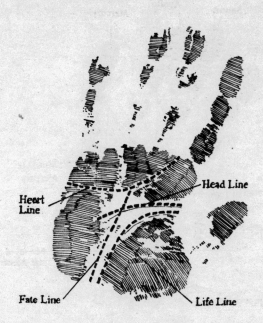

Heart Line

Head Line

Fate Line

Life Line

finger; the career line is the main line below that and the life line runs from the career line all the way down the hand and round the base of the thumb. Don't be worried if lines break on your hand, particularly on the life line as it doesn't necessarily mean you are not going to stay the course!

If the heart line is broken or fragmented this could mean heart trouble or some sort of emotional upheaval. Ideally, the head line should be straight though very few are. The straighter the line the more practical and business-minded you are. If the line drops downwards it is a sign of artistic ability but if it travels upwards it means you have great optimism and seldom get depressed. Lots of lines crossing the life line show that you are a worrier.

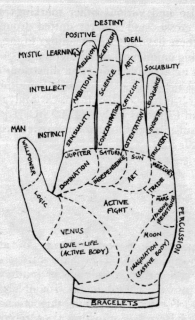

Besides the lines there are plenty of bumps and markings and the palm is like a landscape in itself.

Palmistry's links to astrology are evident in the naming of the mounts on the hand. For instance, the mount just below the first finger is Jupiter, representing ambition; Saturn represents sobriety; Apollo artistic appreciation and talent; and Mercury quick intelligence and optimism. Upper Mars, just below Mercury, shows perseverance, while Lunar along the heel of the hand indicates imagination, intuition and creativity. Venus at the lower base of the thumb is, as you might expect, passion and love, and lastly Lower Mars, above Venus, shows calculation and cunning and coolness. From the centre of the palm is the plane of Mars indicating emotional control, negativity and nervousness.

You will also find various other markings such as circles, stars, crosses and squares dotted around your hand and all these have specific meanings to the trained palmist, showing uniqueness and individuality.

Palmistry is an art with a long and illustrious history. Both Plato and Socrates took it seriously for, although its origins haven't been pinpointed, it was certainly in use in both India and China as early as 3000 BC. Today you will find a palmist in most towns, but particularly in the East and Middle East.

Parapsychology

Parapsychology is the scientific study of abilities, otherwise known as PSI. The main categories are psychokinesis (PK), that is, mind over matter or the ability to see into the environment without use of the physical body. For psychic people this is known as 'tuning in', and it is like adjusting your reception to another person's vibration or another place. The other category of PSI is called Extra-Sensory Perception, or ESP. This is the reception of knowledge beyond your 'normal' senses. Clairvoyance is seeing beyond the physical, while precognition is the knowledge that something is about to happen, and telepathy is direct contact from one mind to another. These are all forms of ESP.

Psychokinesis is also loosely divided into three areas: first, the ability of the mind to influence a moving target such as dice or a shuffle of cards; second, the ability of the mind to move static objects; and third, the ability to influence moving matter such as plant life or animal behaviour. Experiments have proved the existence of clairvoyance and precognition but telepathy has not been so easy to establish in controlled conditions.

Although there is much scepticism about parapsychology and its investigations, the scientific mind has taken giant steps to try to bring the powers of the mind from under the yoke of superstition. The hocus-pocus of the past is at last becoming 'respectable'.

Past-Life Memories

I have remembered the main incidences of all my past lives, so has my husband and so have many of our friends. Yet we have only remembered them when we have *needed* to do so; this has been the case, especially, in connection with relationships with people we're working with. Past-life recall, the way I see it, is not to find out if you've been a king or queen, a saint or sinner, but in order to discover the need for today. A memory that comes up in any particular session is the one that you need to relate to at that moment; it has nothing to do with desire or curiosity. That is simply the way spiritual law works. There has been so much nonsense written about recall of past lives, such as the fact that we come back every two hundred years and incarnate alternatively as men and woman, that I can dismiss it now in one sentence, as nonsense. Everyone is an individual and the number of past lives you have had depends upon that individuality and the need of the time.

The more interesting part of past-life memories is the patterns that come up. If you've been a victim and have been pushed around in most of your lives, you will have acquired an attitude towards this. That pattern is made to be broken and you can, if you wish, change from the victim into the master by simply recognizing the pattern and making a conscious effort of will to rise above it once and for all. The use of power is another interesting pattern, for often, if you've been a leader of the Church or of a country and have misused your power, you find yourself on the receiving end of someone else misusing it.

Then, in a further life, you may find yourself being given a second chance as a leader in order to try again and see if you handle it with more wisdom and understanding. Most people have lives involving magic, witchcraft or what we call following the dark path. These can also be looked upon as experience for often they are of intense value. By remembering negativity we certainly know exactly how positive we really are.

Past-life memories can explain why you have chosen to do the work you are doing, if it was a free choice and you weren't coerced by parents or the educational system! Knowledge of previous talents and gifts can give confidence; for instance, if you feel you would like to heal other people yet do not have the medical training, then the knowledge that you have been a healer or doctor in the past could give you the necessary confidence to pursue this work again. Child prodigies are also a classic example of reincarnation. Mozart, for instance, who wrote his first major composition at the age of seven, is an outstanding example. Many people are disturbed by remembering places they have never been to and this experience is called '*déjà vu*'. Others feel drawn to a particular country in the world that they have never visited, yet will read avidly about its history and origins. It may seem amazing but reincarnation and karma can explain such things. Recalling past lives can clear up phobias such as fear of heights, spiders, birds, cats, clocks, wasps, germs, fire, taking baths, feathers, walking up steps or even seeing a nun cross the street. If this is your problem then this could be the answer for you. I have known of several people cured of the fear of heights by remembering past incidences in other lives when they have either died through falling off a cliff or even by falling through the centre of a windmill. Often a fear of the dark comes from being incarcerated in a cell without light for many hours or even weeks in another time. The strangest phenomena can be explained through recall and can make life much happier and far more secure. A lady with a fear of birds, particularly fluttering birds, was in such terror that it wasn't until she remembered that she had been one of the Christian martyrs tied to a cross and the birds had pecked her eyes out that she could accept the cure. The most important thing to remember about reincarnation and karma is that we all get a second chance. We don't have to feel guilty as many religions would have us believe for we get that second chance whether we deserve it or not.

Another value of a past-life memory is to help you in your present life with the work that you have undertaken. A friend of mine desperately wanted to be a healer but was too self-conscious and nervous to approach anyone and offer them help. By remembering a lifetime when he not only had been a healer but a teacher of healers, he gained that confidence within minutes and gradually became an authority as the knowledge came back into his conscious mind. He now has his own practice and has never looked back. I, myself, have found past-life memories very useful indeed. When I had to address a vast audience at the Planetarium a few years ago, I was shaking in my shoes so much that I'm sure everyone could hear my teeth chatter. Just in time, as I was about to go up the steps to the platform, I remembered that I had been an actress in a recent past life. I simply became that part of myself so much that, when I stood on the stage, I *was* that part of myself. The nerves went and I enjoyed what I was doing. Other friends are making tremendous use of past-life recalls by writing books about the knowledge that is now coming through their conscious minds. One healer that I know is writing a book of the Indian approach to healing, while another friend, a homeopathic doctor, remembers all his past lives as a medicine man and a witch-doctor. My husband, who worked extensively with crystal energies in the past, has brought much of this knowledge through past-life memory. You too can do this and you, too, have a great deal of knowledge to contribute.

Pendulum

Anything can be used as a pendulum from a ring on a piece of cotton to a strangely shaped piece of wood on a length of string, to a beautifully shaped crystal on a silver chain. The pendulum provides an ideal introduction to the psychic sciences because it is so simple to use and gives an immediate proof of natural forces that are not usually seen. Radionic practitioners use a pendulum and so do dowsers who also find water, gold and old coins! How does the pendulum work? It is a telephone link with the subconscious mind; this is the largest part of your mind, a vast memory bank. All impressions and emotions are stored in the subconscious every second of your day and on many levels. This is the link with the universal mind, often called intuition. So you, in fact, are operating the pendulum itself, but on a much deeper level than you are consciously aware.

First of all, get yourself a pendulum, preferably a crystal one that can serve you all your life. Dedicate and programme the crystal to truth, and hold the arm relaxed, grasping the chain or cotton between your forefinger and thumb. Make sure that the arm is sloping slightly downwards, otherwise you won't allow the free flow of the subtle energies. A pendulum moves in three ways: clockwise, anti-clockwise and to and fro, like the pendulum on a clock. Most people find that the pendulum responds to a 'yes' answer clockwise, and a 'no' answer by an anti-clockwise movement. If it swings from north to south like a pendulum on a clock, this means 'maybe' or that you have asked two questions in one. Make sure that your questions are simple and have a 'yes' or 'no' inside your head; address your subconscious mind like an intelligent computer. Having an open and receptive attitude is important for the pendulum won't work if you add your own limitations and don't believe that it will. It moves by muscular movements in the arm so, if you're a stiff, tense person, nothing will happen. The swing of the pendulum is also important for, if it swings in a small swing, it can also swing as wide as it can go. In other words, it is the emphasis that is important. If you ask if you can have cream cakes for tea, and you're on a diet, you could find that the swing is very pronounced. The fun of pendulum working is simply allowing it to happen; you can certainly find out what allergies you have, what foods to eat, or where something is which is lost by holding a pendulum over a map, as well as using it in healing work to find out which part of the body needs help. Diagnosing foods, vitamins and herbs not only benefits you but also benefits those around you. In the past, pendulums were used to discover the sex of eggs, and also the sex of an unborn child – the pendulum here was often a wedding ring on a piece of cotton. Perhaps your grandmother did this? I know that my grandmother, Dorothy did, although more often than not she used a darning needle!

Pentagram

This is a five-pointed star which represents the highest power of spirituality. It is often considered with two points facing downwards as the symbol of man; the two lower points represent the feet standing on the earth, the two horizontal points are the arms outstretched and the point at the top is the head reaching up to the heavens. This is also a symbol of protection and is used a great deal in magic.

The pentagram also represents the four elements, earth, air, fire and water plus a fifth factor – the ruling spirit. It is said to be most effective if it is placed within a circle. In the middle ages it was used a great deal as a symbol to protect the home and to stop goods and loved ones being taken away. There are no statistics to show that, if you wear one, you are less likely to be burgled, however!

Phrenology

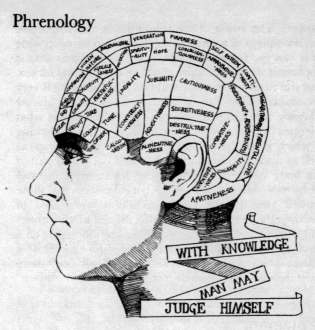

WITH KNOWLEDGE

MAN MAY

JUDGE HIMSELF

This is the study of the shape and contours of the human head, and is said to show your character and personality. Phrenologists say there is a correlation between the shapes and contours and your mental faculty and potential. It hasn't been proved that there is any relationship between the bumps on the head and the brain, in any physical sense, and the fact that you have a large skull or a small one with certain bumps and bulges is no reflection on your brain power. Very popular in Victorian times, phrenology has achieved some results though it is extremely rare now to find a phrenologist in your neighbourhood. It is said that particular areas of the skull show how spiritual you are, how idealistic, how courageous and how hopeful and also whether you have the ability to be a linguist, a mathematician or are musically inclined or like art. It is thought that strength and weaknesses can be shown and then a total analysis of your character deduced. I have never yet met a phrenologist as they seem to be extremely rare, but I would be most interested to hear if you have ever had this done yourself.

Poltergeist

If you have ever experienced poltergeist activity you will be in no doubt as to what it is. A poltergeist is usually mischievous, making inexplicable noises such as the slamming of doors, loud knockings and rappings and the smashing of crockery or glass with no obvious physical cause. Sometimes pools of water occur or spontaneous fires and there can even be marks, scratches and writing on walls and floors. The moving of heavy furniture or tables sailing through the air have also been reported.

Here is an example of uncontrolled mediumship that needs to be directed. A sensitive will be able to correct this and, should this happen in your experience, do seek help as quickly as possible. This is no time to pray to St Christopher to find whatever is missing, so do take the poltergeist activity for what it is!

Poltergeist activity usually occurs when there is a young teenager in the house as, under certain conditions of mental strain, it seems that some partial deflection of the inner energies of the teenager can take place. It is as if subconscious telepathic impulses are sent out charged with inner energies, and it is this that causes physical manifestations such as the movement of objects across a room. Certainly, most of the reported cases can be traced to this and, as soon as the teenager grows up or the case is investigated, then the activity seems to cease. Occasionally, pools of water appear and showers of small stones, but it is very seldom that anyone is really hurt by these boisterous activities.

Power of Thought and Thought-Forms

'The thoughts that come often unsought,
and, as it were, drop into the mind, are
commonly the most valuable of any we have.'

John Locke

Every aspect of human life is the power of thought for thought is infinite. Thought influences your life from birth to death and, in fact, all philosophy, arts, science and all forms of invention, healing and indeed life itself are the result of real thought. It is only when you limit your thoughts and your own attitude of mind that you fail to achieve true creativity.

The power of the intellect and of the mind is tremendous but, of the two, the mind is far more powerful than any intellect. Even though our normal functioning power involves the intellect, thought energies penetrate outwards in your mind and spread to wherever you can push them or allow them to go, whether you are conscious of this or not. Consequently, you create quite a force around you and in your environment. Most of the time, these thoughts are of a very mild nature, but they can gradually build up a force over a long period of time. Therefore, your thoughts about your house, school or job, make a place for you, and you start to create the environment that you need to be conducive to what you want to do. Everything around you that you call modern, is due to somebody thinking about it and creating it, and is also due to your own collective thought forces coming together and helping these things manifest. You are what you eat, but you are also what your environment is; therefore, any violence, anger or fear in you is reflected in society, for it is your thought force that supports and helps these things to grow.

Not all thoughts are negative, of course, for there are also great and beautiful things in your environment towards which you also make a contribution. Obviously,

167

it is much more beneficial to yourself and to those around you and your environment, to have positive and constructive thoughts and to become much more harmonious. Very precise thoughts can either come from the higher intellect or, if they are extremely intense, can result from anger, passion or hate. Such thoughts are so powerful that they take form. They not only move very fast, but they attach themselves and hang on with a great deal of suction to the person or situation and are very real. If you send out a powerful thought to a sensitive person, they will feel it. If it is a violent thought, it is just like striking them with your fist. If it is a selfish one, it is received as a feeling of hanging on to the skin and clothes. If it is a hurtful one it is like saying something to them within, so that they can hear it. Even if the person is not sensitive, the energies from your thought still surrounds them and makes them feel strange or uncomfortable.

You can, of course, also receive thoughts from other people and thought forces that have the same effect on you. If you are walking into a room full of anger, you can feel it, feel the thoughts and feel it coming off people. If you go into an environment that is harmonious and constructive, it has the same effect on you and makes you feel positive and optimistic. You *are* what you think as well as what you eat. Do remember that.

Most of us have no idea just how powerful our thoughts are, or even that they can be seen by psychics as shapes and colours. Thoughts of love and highly spiritual thoughts often appear blue and purple with curved outlines, but thoughts of anger, hate and fear form barbed arrows and can be scarlet, green, and even black. Guarding your thoughts is all-important, for they can really affect those close to you. This is one reason why prayer is so powerful for an intense concentration of thought sent to a particular person in a loving way can be extremely protective and reassuring. Unfortunately, the reverse is also true. It is also possible to build up definite forms on the inner levels by the power of thought, and these forms may well persist as a kind of separate object, attached to people or objects. A novelist, writing a book, can create the characters as thought-forms and we often hear from such people that their characters took on a life of their own. The blessing of the Christian cross or any other object used in a religious way can also be charged with energies of thought-forms. Talismans will also come in this category, for anyone who wears one or comes into contact with it will experience emotions similar to those of the thought-form with which it was charged. It is, therefore, important to know where your jewellery came from, as such things may be a link to the person who made or charged them.

Your thoughts can really change the world. All too often people say, 'What can *I* do in a world that is so chaotic and heading for self-destruction?' What you can do, however, is to raise your own consciousness and make sure your own thought force is used constructively. Sitting quietly and spending five minutes every day of your life, sending out thoughts of love, peace and sharing will link you with other people doing just the same, for this produces the wonderful light, like a beacon, that will touch even the hardest heart. Instead of condemning, criticizing and judging, send out thoughts of peace and harmony. Those who misuse you and hurt you are often very hurt inside themselves, so be compassionate and surround them with thoughts of love and caring. A whole new, harmonious and happy world will be yours as a result.

The medical profession and scientists are becoming increasingly aware of the power of the mind. Only recently has it been discovered that only one fifth of the mind is used. It is quite possible to heal yourself by sheer willpower and the will to live or the will to die is in our own hands or, rather, our heads. Terminal illnesses can be reversed by willpower and thought power. It is simply up to you. Positive thoughts travel like bright, white lights while bad and negative thoughts linger like a grey mist. Some people feel gloomy and seem to have a cloud around their heads, while others simply shine with vitality and enthusiasm. By thinking positively you attract positive thought waves to yourself and, of course, the converse is true. Negative thinking can actually produce such a black cloud that you are in a 'black' mood.

It is often the power of thought that works miracles. Try to develop your awareness because only by so doing can you raise your consciousness to new levels of thought and belief. Heightened awareness increases sensitivity and you will become a far more positive person. You can create a better life by being aware and thinking well of others and of yourself. Increase the power of thought by deep breathing and visualization. Set aside your five minutes each day and see the changes.

Prayer

Prayer is a request to the deity or object of worship, offering your reverence or, more often, asking for help to solve a problem, or keep you in their safe keeping.

The idea of prayer goes back to antiquity and was probably due to man needing to control the forces of nature so that he would survive. The fear of not being able to control things led to the idea of talking to, and negotiating with, forces of nature in their different forms. Prayer, worship and sacrifices, based on fear and respect, have developed in a variety of forms in every country in the world. In Iran the word 'Yaz' means both prayer and sacrifice and this two-way approach is also expressed in the Old Testament in Psalm 5, verse 3: 'O Lord in the morning thou dose hear my voice, in the morning I prepare a sacrifice for thee and watch.'

Sacrifices, like prayer, are dictated to some extent by

the needs of the god or goddess that is being approached. When a request for help to a deity is involved it seems that nourishment as well as honour needs to be bestowed upon them for the best results. In many countries of the world, prayer and sacrifices, not necessarily blood ones, are the standard approach to God. In your local church bread and wine symbolize the sacrifices Jesus made, and the money tray is your sacrifice. Flowers, incense, fruit and especially made artefacts and animals are all sacrifices that people make in the hope that their deity or god will provide them with whatever they are asking for.

The words of the prayers that accompany this approach are extremely important and, while many prayers invite the deity to consider the problem and provide its help, this is not always the case. In many religious practices the prayer becomes more like a spell which conjures up and forms a direct control over the deity. This is only done when approaching the demi-gods, for the Supreme God is recognized and respected in every religion in the world. In many countries prayers or mantras, which are sounds of power, are repeated over and over again; this results in the person entering into a trance-like state which separates him from the normal state of consciousness. When this is achieved communication between man and God is much clearer and much more direct. The Buddhists in Tibet use a prayer wheel which is a revolving cylindrical box inscribed with prayers and mantras. The repetition of the mantras or the turning of the wheel is a way of conveying a blessing to the deity. The Navaho Indians have a prayer stick which is made from special wood, with feathers, shells and sacred objects attached to it. The sticks are placed arround the site of the ceremony and serve as invitations to the deity or other beings. The power of the sticks and the magical objects involved in the ceremony is reinforced by special songs and prayers. If everything is done according to custom the gods have no choice but to come! Here we can see the fine line in approaches to prayer as to whether you ask or command the help of the deity.

In your everyday life you may see no need to approach God to help you in your affairs, but this soon changes when you are in real trouble or somebody close to you has a problem which you cannot alleviate. Then all the stops come out and privately, sometimes even secretly, the asking emerges in half-forgotten prayers from your childhood. This form of communication is instinctive and comes from the depths of your being because it is a fundamental part of your psyche. Primitive man is still lurking around inside you and, when the rational modern world cannot help you, you have no alternative but to look towards more infinite powers.

The best-known prayer in Christian countries is probably the Lord's Prayer which has a wide range of requests and also pays reverence to God. This creates an extremely powerful energy when it is spoken or thought. It pays reverence to the Father and asks his help so that we can find our daily bread; asks forgiveness and the strength to forgive others and also asks that we be not led into temptation so that we will be delivered from evil, giving us a better chance of having a clear life, here on earth and in Heaven.

The idea that God is not only looking after you, but is also directly concerned about your destiny is probably one of the most comforting thoughts you can rely on when you fear something or need help. When you are in trouble, or disturbed about something, try not only to use prayers to something that is exterior, but also look inside yourself and see what it is that you are not understanding or accepting. The total effect of your prayer will have a much wider and more profound effect upon the situation if you take responsibility for the situation and guide the forces from within and without to bring about a solution to the problem. The most beautiful scene in reference to a prayer is that of a child saying his prayers with sincerity and innocence before he goes to bed. The following prayer is one many of us know and probably even remember from our childhood:

> Now I lay me down to sleep, I pray the Lord my soul to keep,
> And if I die before I wake, I pray The Lord my soul to take.

and another lovely one is:

> Gentle Jesus, meek and mild,
> Look upon a little child,
> Pity my simplicity,
> Suffer me to come to Thee.

Prophecy

This is a Greek word meaning 'speaking before' and does, of course, concern a forecast of events yet to come. It is not quite the same as fortune telling or divination as, in biblical times, prophets were not only seers of the future but also direct representatives or spokesmen for God. Such prophets advised kings and courts and, throughout the Old Testament, the words 'came to pass' occur frequently. A prophet, such as Jeremiah, forecast Israel's destruction but prophets didn't always forecast doom and disaster. The prophet Daniel saw the rise and fall of kings and kingdoms, including the nation of Israel. Elijah and Moses were also prophets as was Joseph of the many-coloured coat, who warned of the seven years of plenty and the seven years of famine. In the New Testament John the Baptist was the forerunner and the prophet. It was he who announced that 'someone will come after me who is greater than I'.

Throughout history prophets have flourished and although, in the Bible, the prophets were usually men, in Greece and Rome they were mostly women. The Delphic Oracle, Pythia, was a priestess and a virgin. In Egypt and other Middle Eastern countries the seers were also women. Roger Bacon, during the Dark Ages, had a burst of prophecy and talked about 'ocean-going ships and aeroplanes'. He also prophesied the microscope and the telescope but it wasn't until two centuries later in Italy that Leonardo da Vinci came up with the blueprint. Michel de Nostredame is probably the world's best-known prophet.

Michel de Nostredame, who later used the latinized form of his name, Nostradamus, lived during the sixteenth century, yet his prophecies covered a five-century span. Out of the thousand major predictions of world events that he made during his lifetime, so far 800 of these have proved to be accurate and have come true.

This extraordinary French astrologer and prophet wrote the most amazing book, *Centuries*, in which he foretold the coming of plagues, wars and world disasters. It is written in such an obscure and enigmatic way, however, that it is often misunderstood and this, in itself, perpetuates the mysteries of fortune telling.

Nostradamus even predicted his own death in 1577 and the date when his remains would be moved to another resting place. He has prophesied that London won't exist in its present form after 1986. Nostradamus predicts a third world war that will take place in the northern hemisphere after two great powers join in an alliance against the East. He says:

When those of the Northern Pole
Are united together
In the East will be great fear and dread. . .
One day the two great leaders
   will be friends.
The new land will be at the
   height of its power;
To the man of blood the number is repeated. . .

The new land has been translated as America (which had not even been discovered in his lifetime) and the man of blood is interpreted as referring to the third anti-Christ who will emerge in China. This prediction, therefore, suggests a coming war between China and a Russian-American alliance. He even goes on to give an exact date, 1999 and seven months. All is not lost, however, for he also predicted that mankind would survive and start the great cycle of life again.

It is well worth looking at Nostradamus's quatrains.

In more modern times, at the turn of this century, the American, Edgar Cayce, became famous as the Sleeping Prophet. Cayce's prophecies go up to the period 1998. Not only did he produce thousands of personal forecasts about the health and careers of individuals who consulted him, but he also predicted long-range geological changes of continental magnitude. His prophecies included a 'breakup in the western portion of America', and changes 'in the upper portion of Europe' while 'the greater portion of Japan must go into the sea'.

Jean Dixon who lives in Washington DC is a modern-day dramatic prophet, and has predicted correctly several election results and the death of the President John F. Kennedy, assassinated in Dallas on 22 November 1963. She forsees peace in 1999, although she does see a world holocaust. In the 1980s a new world leader emerges from the Middle East and brings the peace that is so desired.

Not all prophets are so successful or accurate and there are many today who regularly give out information that is really off-beam. As the apostle Matthew said:

Beware of false prophets, which come to you in sheep's clothing, but inwardly they are ravening wolves.

Matthew 7:15

It certainly takes courage to be a modern-day prophet, as the disciple John says a prophet is often:

'The voice of one crying in the wilderness.'

John 1:23

How do you know if a prophecy is true? Tune into your heart centre and your intuitive sense. See if it *feels* right to you. Besides that, of course, only time will tell!

Psychic Self-Defence

From experience I have found that the people who are most open to psychic attack are those who attract fear to themselves.

It is extraordinary that most people safeguard themselves against all sorts of things; for instance, you take out insurance to guard against being burgled, against having your car stolen or against accidents or travel mishaps, but who takes out an insurance against psychic attack? Bolting and locking your doors and windows does not stop thought-forms from hurting you or entities from making your life miserable. Chain letters received through the post can be a form of psychic attack for these are usually anonymous and like poison-pen letters, they depend on your response and the fear that you feel when you receive them. Drop them in the waste bin immediately or put them on the fire! Many psychic attacks are produced by sheer power of thought so, if you feel that someone is attacking you, look around and see who is being jealous, suspicious, malicious or greedy, and check your friends who may have been dabbling in occult experiences such as seances, astral projection or even exorcism without proper training or knowledge. Often people venture into dimensions where the forces that are encountered are not ones they recognize, let alone control. This can be quite dangerous and is very foolhardy.

Most low-level psychic phenomena result from unhappiness and ignorance projected in the form of negative thoughts by the living. These thoughts do not need a ghost or ghoul for the living can haunt just as effectively by these means. You may be the sort of person that attracts ghosts and a great deal depends on your own disposition and attitude. If you're a happy-go-lucky person with an outsize sense of humour, it is not likely that a ghost will be able to manifest too strongly. I heard a story recently of a house in south London which was haunted. The first people who had the house were very kind, unassuming, gentle folk who were terrified by the tall, dark man on the stairs, and the more they showed their terror the more he appeared. Eventually, they left. The next family was full of life and vitality and they simply saw the whole thing as a huge joke and were never, ever bothered by it, and never ever saw the ghost. When they eventually moved, a family like the first one took over and the same thing happened as with the first family. The haunting kept on and on until they moved out. Humour is a wonderful policy! Of the many people that I have encountered who have tried to look horrific and devilish, I have only had to say to them, 'You're an illusion and I don't believe in you,' and actually laugh at them, to disperse them totally. Mind you, you have to believe this and not have your heart knocking inside your chest at a mile a minute! There is no doubt that you can become ill through psychic attack because so much tension and unpleasant feelings build up when thought-forms are directed at you in a poisonous way. You may not even realize what is happening for often the cause won't be obvious at first.

If you're attacked, what do you do? The first thing is not to panic and the second is to try to find an experienced sensitive to help you. Controlling your own thoughts is essential for, if you're as positive and as loving as you can be, this is a wonderfully protective measure. Few of us use our natural energy to the full and this natural energy is in the aura for our protection. If you're worried, anxious or fearful, your aura is affected and you'll need to nurture and nourish it as much as the physical body. Imagine a colour that feels good to you, like blue or indigo, or even pure white radiating light, and see yourself surrounded by it. By consciously controlled mental effort, keep away all negativity and inharmonious thoughts. Surround yourself with beauty and harmony, read inspiring books and listen to uplifting music. I particularly like the Hallelujah chorus from 'The Messiah'. Above all, remember that the power of love is the greatest power that you have at your command and, by returning this energy towards whatever is being sent to you, you can reverse the situation. It works every time.

Psychic Surgery

Psychic surgery is a roaring trade in the Philippines and, although several investigations have proved some practitioners to be fraudulent, others do seem to gain benefit from it. The most interesting case of such a phenomenon concerns a Brazilian named Arigo who had little schooling and worked as a farmhand. When he was thirty he became depressed, had nightmares and sleepwalking sessions. A local spiritualist told him that a spirit was trying to work through him. Arigo became a healer and was seeing as many as 300 patients a day. In one case, a psychic researcher from America had a tumour removed from his arm in less than five seconds. A hundred people stood around to witness it and a camera crew recorded the event. Arigo took a pocket knife, held the American's arm and wielded the knife. The next thing the American remembers is the tumour from his arm being placed in his hand along with the pocket knife. He had been completely conscious and felt no pain although his arm was bleeding. The film showed that Arigo had made a gesture of cutting the skin twice and, on doing so, the skin had split wide open revealing the tumour. Arigo just squeezed the tumour and it popped out. The incision was only covered with a sticking plaster and, after three days, the wound was healed. Arigo performed hundreds of other operations the same way and gave accurate diagnoses of illnesses. He could also estimate blood pressure accurately without the use of instruments and gave complex drug remedies. He said that he arrived at the diagnoses by listening to the voice in his right ear and repeating whatever it said. The voice was his spirit guide, a German medical student who had died a long time ago. Sadly, Arigo died in a car crash in 1971 leaving a remarkable and well-documented case of psychic ability to tease the scientists.

Many who operate psychic surgery, however, are fraudulent and you should remember this if you ever have cause to seek such help.

Psychokinesis

This has been widely publicized during the last few years by Uri Geller and is the ability to cause metal to bend by apparently non-physical means. Uri says that he wills it to bend and therefore this is another 'thought-form'. He strokes a fork or spoon in such a way that the molecular structure alters under his touch. Suffice to say he's not unique in this and, when appearing on television, thousands of people found they had the same ability and thousands of clocks also stopped at the same time. Again, I ask, what is the point of it all? It's very difficult to eat with a bent spoon or fork and, besides demonstrating the phenomenon, has it any practical or useful value in our world today?

Psychokinetic Energy

Psychokinetic energy is produced by the mind and is believed to be capable of affecting things in the environment by consciously or unconsciously willing it to be so. Your mind is a very powerful tool and it transmits energy all the time. Some of these energies can be so strong that they affect the physical objects around you or cause things to happen that should not normally occur. There is an increase in the energy when you are agitated or angry and it can be directed towards somebody in a very precise way. Often you may only have a passing thought and yet the feeling seems to happen immediately after this thought has occurred. The release of psycho-kinetic energy travels with the speed of thought, and its effects can be instantaneous.

In laboratory-controlled conditions, a Russian called Nina Kulagin has been seen to cause painful burns on human skin, move objects and stop the heart of a frog, all by concentrating her mental energy on the objects. There are other reports of people dispersing clouds, causing electrical faults, moving objects off the ground, and making things disappear and reappear in different locations. Most poltergeist activity has also been found to be the result of psychokinetic energies. This energy has been considered hocus-pocus for a long time but, in the last fifty years, scientific study has produced a great deal of evidence to suggest that the mind is capable of doing such things.

For the mystics, psychics and healers of this world, this energy is the basic tool used to help them in their work. Remember, though, that everyone produces this energy and it can have a constructive or destructive effect on you and your environment. When you are angry or violent, mentally or physically, you intensify the output of this energy and it has an effect on the person that you are directing it towards. There is a story of a clairvoyant who was in a pub during an argument between a husband and wife; when the argument reached boiling point the man got up to hit his wife. The clairvoyant saw a bolt of lightning hit the wife before she was physically struck. There are also many people who care and send out gentleness and love; this can also have a tremendous effect on relationships and the environment. One such story is about Gandhi who had the thought that non-violent passive resistance could take apart the hold that the British had on his country. In an extraordinary exhibition of self-discipline and understanding, he directed the collective energy of such an idea, captured the imagination of the whole world and brought about the desired change. On a day-to-day basis, you can do the same. If you are in conflict with somebody, don't send anger or violence towards him, instead sit down quietly and picture him in your mind, see what the conflict is all about, not trying to force it one way or another. Then visualize the conflict being resolved and the problems that created the situation sorting them-selves out. When somebody is ill or upset, don't just sit and worry about it, visualize the person in a good state of health and condition, and make available your love and strength if needed. This may sound crazy, but this type of activity can bring about astounding results because your mind is capable of producing energy that can affect other people and exterior objects. It has been used for thousands of years and everybody is capable of using and producing it in any way they wish. Obviously use these energies in a sensible way, and do be careful for, if you transmit selfish and clinging energies, your life will only consist of such things and eventually they will suffocate you. On the other hand, if you transmit sharing and caring your life will be full of these types of energies because you really do reap what you sow.

Psychometry

Most people have held a family heirloom or looked through an antique shop and picked up one or two pieces that have attracted their eye, and felt a sensation from them. Sometimes it is sadness or sometimes joy, but you can also have feelings of loneliness, loss and even horror.

Family heirlooms are often prized for their sentimental value and many date back hundreds of years. Because they have been given with love from generation to generation they have a tremendous aura of love attached to them.

Holding an object in your hand and and sensing it, is what psychometry is all about; it is the ability to experience that object in a feeling sense. It is important also, if you're buying antique jewellery, that you sense the energy of the person who has had it before you and, if it is uncomfortable, then either refuse the piece or simply cleanse it in your own mind before you wear it. You can do this by the power of thought and simply will love and caring into the piece to overcome the existing emotion attached to it. It is possible to psychometrize almost anything from a piece of material, a piece of paper, to a crystal or a rock. Some results can be extremely detailed and minutely accurate and the word picture astonishing. The police are often helped tremendously by psychometrists when they are hunting for missing persons or trying to chase a murder victim, for the help that can be given in this way by a sensitive has been proved time and time again to be accurate. Yet anyone can develop this ability for it is simply allowing the intuitive mind, the feeling side of you, to sense what is in your hand. Closing the eyes certainly helps and you will, after a little practice, have a feeling or sensation that could amaze you. My husband was given a piece of wood by a writer friend to psychometrize; he was not only able to establish that it was from a Viking ship but also that it was part of the hull. He also pinpointed where the ship was now and how it got there.

My husband, the intrepid metal detector, found a beautiful little carved ebony elephant in the mud of the River Thames. We thought it would be interesting to psychometrize it. Not only did we see an urchin throw it into the Thames but we also back-tracked its history beyond that. We saw a Victorian carriage and a small boy and his governess driving along the Embankment and the small boy had the elephant clutched in his hand. In a fit of temper he threw it out of the window and the urchin subsequently picked it up. Taking it even further back, it was one of a set of five that the small boy kept in his nursery. We could see the room quite distinctly and this was the smallest elephant of the set. My husband has also psychometrized about twenty different rings that he has also found embedded in the mud of the Thames by metal-detecting. Many of them had been stolen from their owners and the burglars had extracted the stones from the rings and thrown them over a bridge or the embankment walls. Again we could trace back to the original owner and also pick up the mood and feeling that accompanied the jewellery.

How do you psychometrize? Like many skills there is a certain knack in being able to take hold of an object belonging to somebody else and telling them about themselves, their lives and any past associations, from the object in your hand. You will certainly need patience as well as a degree of sensitivity to be able to read such objects. When you first hold a ring, for instance, feel it first with the left hand and then with both hands. Does it feel hot or cold? Is there an impression of an emotional state? Try to be as precise as possible and don't waffle. Remember you are not using the part of your mind that is used in everyday life and you have to be relaxed and detached in outlook. The more detached you are the clearer the images will be and the easier it will be to focus on the ring. The temptation is to think things out but, if you do this, you will lose your intuitive sense and come to a very abrupt stop. You may pick up all kinds of feelings, perceptions and pictures and it could seem quite a muddle when you begin, but persevere and you will soon find the knack of holding the object and being in the correct state of mind.

Psychometry can be quite a useful skill. For instance, you can learn a lot about antique furniture or art or go to the local museum and probe into the exhibits through your own sense of touch. It will take time to master this art but it can have quite an effect in everyday life. If you go to a jumble sale you will know exactly who has worn that jumper, or, if you pick up a vase in a secondhand shop, you will know its history. Every time you shake hands with someone you will also pick up much about that person as well. This will certainly give you a social advantage, if nothing more!

The only problem with psychometry is that it is possible for the psychic to pick up vibrations from a previous owner, particularly if it is a second-hand piece of jewellery, and, although you may find this fascinating, it is not always helpful. On the other hand, if you receive a piece of jewellery that belonged to someone else, it might be a good idea to find out what memories and feelings are already attached to it. Hopefully they are all of happiness and love!

Pyramid Power

There are pyramids in Peru, Central America and Egypt. Attached to them is much mystery, fantasy, legend and conjecture, all of which continue to intrigue all those who try to find the answers. Who built the pyramids? For what purpose? And where did the builders acquire the extraordinarily advanced scientific and astronomical knowledge?

One of the remaining seven wonders of the world is the Great Pyramid of Giza, a short camel ride from Cairo. Edgar Cayce, the American psychic, said in one of his readings that it was built over 10,000 years ago by non-Egyptians and that it wasn't a tomb but a storage place for the history of mankind from the very beginning up to the year 1998. This history is written in the language of mathematics, geometry and astronomy. Literally, the Great Pyramid is a library in stone. Within the halls, rooms and passages measurements have been found that correspond in time to momentous historical events, except that they were prophesied rather than simply recorded. Such things as the Great Flood, the birth of Jesus, the date of the Crucifixion, outstanding wars and the development of religions. The two world wars are accurately prophesied. Not only do the Great Pyramid dimensions correspond to the polar diameter and radius of the earth but they also accurately correspond to the measurements in time and movement of the equinoxes and the solar year. The Great Pyramid has been shown by engineers and mathematicians to embody the value for Pi (π). Not only was the yearly calendar of 365 days being used at that time, but the perimeter of the base of the pyramid was an exact fraction of the circumference of the earth.

A pyramid shape itself contains much power and there has been a great deal of research in recent years about this. Many people experiment by putting razor blades under a pyramid shape, only to find they are sharpened the next day. This is to do with the arrangement of the molecules within the razor blade; the pyramid causes regeneration of the edge material. Putting pyramid-shaped food covers over your perishable food will preserve it far longer than any other method. Try putting a half-eaten apple under a pyramid shape and you will see that is won't decay so quickly. You can turn grapes into raisins, fresh mushrooms into dried mushrooms and so on. What you must do, however, is align the pyramid to the true geographic north and south axis. To make the experiment viable keep the second half of the apple, for instance, outside the pyramid. It can take a while to preserve foodstuffs – sometimes as much as eight weeks – but the foodstuffs, such as mushrooms, taste just like fresh ones, and keep their colour. Herbs can also be treated in this way. If you want to give an ailing plant a boost hang the pyramid cone about twelve inches over it and it will soon perk up.

Simply sitting in a large pyramid shape can be very healing. Several people have experimented with this most successfully. It can also be an energy booster. James Coburn, the film star, is reported to have said that he believes in pyramid power and that, when he crawls inside his pyramid tent, sitting in a yoga position, it really does work. He finds it gives off a definite feeling and sensation and even creates an atmosphere that makes it easier to meditate, closing out all interference. It is possible to sleep inside a pyramid shape and those who have done so reach a deeper sleeping state than before. The reactions that you are likely to get are tingly feelings, flushes of colour, prickly sensations, a sense of music and increased sense perception. It is well worth experimenting with the pyramid shape in this way to see what it does for you. Colours are also effective, so do your own experiments and see what happens.

There is no doubt that we are getting knowledgeable about pyramid energy. There is a huge pyramid-shaped skyscraper in San Francisco and a church in Texas, besides pyramid-shaped houses and even pyramid shaped hats! Perhaps we'll soon have pyramid supermarkets and pyramid healing centres. There is no doubt that being in a pyramid shape has a very relaxing effect and can boost the energy levels. Perhaps we ought to try childbirth inside a pyramid tent. Certainly, several experimenters have found that negative feelings and headaches are eliminated and even more adventurous ones find love-making ecstatic!

Pyromancy

This is a form of divination using fire. People who practise pyromancy interpret the way the fire burns and the movement of the flames. Apparently, the person for whom the guidance is required is fixed in the seer's mind and then herbs, twigs, leaves or incense are thrown upon the fire and the reactions in the fire, such as the colour of the flame, the amount of smoke and the increase or decrease of the burning, are watched and then interpreted. Another way of fortune telling by fire is the candle flame or the flame of an oil-lamp. Again, the reactions of the flame – how it flickers or flares, together with any sputtering or colour changes – are watched and interpreted. Pyromancy may be, basically, commonsense for, if the candle flame burns brighter it is obviously an optimistic and hopeful sign, whereas, if it dies down, perhaps you ought to forget the whole thing!

Qabalah

The Qabalah is like a giant filing cabinet full of knowledge, inner wisdom and secret law, connected with the occult and magical doctrine. It is a philosophical system that believes that a part of the spirit of God 'fell' through ten planes of existence into a lower state of consciousness. The human world is supposed to be the lowest of the ten, although it is believed that man has, within, the seed of divinity, and therefore it is possible to raise himself to the stage where he can be in harmony with the entire universe, otherwise known as God.

The vehicle that is provided to accomplish this task is a type of ladder, known as the Tree of Life. The tree is seen as ten spheres and, when combined, will represent all that exists in the universe. At the top is Kether – the crown of God, followed by Reshith – male god of wisdom, Hesed – love and mercy, Netsah – endurance, Dinah – female understanding and intelligence, Gedurah – power, Hod – majesty, Tifereth – beauty, Tesod – active force, and Mankhuth – kingdom or universe. The left-hand pillar represents the female, receptive principle and the right-hand pillar represents the male or creative principle while the middle pillar is the balancing factor between the two.

The journey on the Tree of Life is not as straightforward as you might think, for it involves touching upon all the links between man, nature, mental, mystical and spiritual laws. The journey is a slow and laborious struggle, twisting from one side of the tree to another

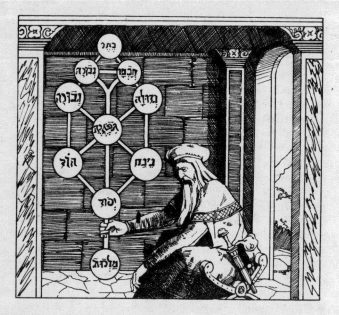

with dead ends and false paths. When you consider it, you are doing this throughout your life, and the Tree of Life can be translated into your own struggles, thoughts and feelings, because your life itself is a journey taking you from one stage of development to the next. The Tree of Life shows that the struggle has been recognized and the structure has been devised so you can climb the tree and, although you might not understand all the jargon, you are climbing your own tree of life, the way back to being in touch with your own spiritual self.

Reincarnation and Karma

Since the beginning of recorded history the question has arisen time and time again, 'What happens when we die?' In the teachings of the great religions as well as in the testimonies of numerous masters, such as the Buddha and Jesus Christ, and legions of prophets and seers of all ages and races: 'There is no death!'

The teachings of the masters and their very lives would become meaningless if this were not so; as would the work and evidence of every spiritualist and psychic living today. During the last six centuries there is also the recorded testimony of all the ancient schools of spiritual thought as well as all great world religions, although many of the early teachings of those religions have been altered or lost and the idea of reincarnation has been discarded.

Today, however, this can be reaffirmed by anyone who is interested enough and there is plenty of scientific research and evidence to support it. There are many books on the market which list after-death experiences by those who have suffered accident or heart attack or some such incident and have experienced 'life on the other side' and then returned back to the body to relate their story.

Each time you live a life on earth you incarnate and the soul enters a new body. Each time you die you discard that body like a suit of old clothes and reincarnate into a new one. Everyone has an immeasurably long past during which, by trial and error, in ignorance or in growing understanding, life after life, they have been slowly and often painfully growing and learning. There is no doubt that the quality of future life is somehow related to the quality of the life that preceeded death. Yet, looking around us, it seems as if some are more blessed than others. It is important to remember that your present life is of your own making for, whether you acknowledge it or not, every past act is your own responsibility and every past deed will determine your next life and the circumstances you choose for yourself.

Understanding reincarnation also means an understanding of karma, for karma is the state that we create for ourselves as a result of our actions in this life and other lives. Karma is the key to reincarnation and, literally, the word means action! Karma is the spiritual law of cause and effect and there is no cause that, sooner or later, does not show itself in an effect; and there is no event or circumstance that is not the effect of a past cause. You are master of your own destiny! Yet the old idea of good being rewarded and evil being punished may not be immediately apparent. Each single act needs to be worked out during successive lifetimes until you understand the consequences of all your actions. Each lifetime produces a credit of good deeds as well as hurtful ones and in some lives the balance can be undoubtedly evil. Above all, it is necessary to learn that it is the quality of life that counts.

'So who was I?' Most people enjoy imagining glamorous associations and see themselves as a famous person, a king or a queen, a swashbuckling pirate or great artist or poet. Recently, there was a party in Hollywood called 'Come As You Were'. It was interesting to note there were several queens of Spain (all of the same name) as well as more than two Cleopatras and Joans of Arc! Shallow curiosity is one thing but it is not knowledge. Obviously, not everyone was a member of a royal family or a prophet; after all, think of the foot soldiers, the people who died in the plagues and those who cleaned out the latrines. It is possible that, if you misused wealth in one life and were a person of great estate and importance, you would choose the lesson in the next life of being a beggar and understanding the value of material goods and their responsibility.

Child genius is evidence of reincarnation. Occasionally, certain children have the most amazing talents

which obviously could not be learnt in the normal way. Mozart, at the age of three years, started taking music lessons from his father and, at the age of six years, toured Germany giving harpsichord recitals. When he was seven years old he not only played the harpsichord, violin and organ but also composed for all three instruments. At ten years old he wrote an oratorio and at eleven years wrote a comic opera. This was at an age when children do not have a sense of humour. At the amazing age of fourteen he had taken his composer's degree at the Academy of Music and had his first opera successfully produced in Milan. Here is an irresistably convincing picture of ready-made knowledge, skill and experience carried over from a very recent previous incarnation. The very interesting question is, who was he before that? Another child prodigy was Michaelangelo, the giant among sculptors and artists, born in 1475. By the time he was eleven years old he was painting more brilliantly than his teachers and his pictures were sold with his signature. By the time he was thirteen years old he was acknowledged as a genius in his own right and his enormous output during his very short life meant he came into the world equipped with a ready-made and unforgotten skill. I am sure there are many children today who show such remarkable talents. Obviously, the interval of time between death and rebirth can happen within days rather than years; the pattern of a former life is carried over practically intact in certain cases, with only the memory of events being more or less obliterated. Who do you know?

Many great souls have tried to depict reincarnation; these include Wagner, the German composer, and William Blake, the poetic genius.

Perhaps the best epitaph ever written is by Benjamin Franklin. He wrote it for himself at the age of twenty-two.

The Body of B. Franklin,
    Printer
Like the cover of an old book,
Its contents torn out
    And
Stripped of its lettering and guidling,
    Lies here
Food for Worms
But the book shall not be lost,
For it will as he believed
Appear once more
In a new and more elegant edition
Revised and corrected
    By the author.

Reincarnation opens the door through which there is hope and light, and the laws of the universe and nature begin to make an understandable pattern.

It is easy to see karma at work in everyday life for no one's life fits a logical pattern. However well laid your plans and however ambitious and dedicated you are in achieving them, nothing happens to order. Every day successful people lose fortunes whilst dishonest folk prosper; or those who have led apparently blameless lives develop terminal diseases or suffer tragedy. Is this luck or is this karma? The Old Testament adage of an eye for an eye and a tooth for a tooth is not necessarily meant in a physical sense. If you murder someone and chop his head off with an axe in one life it's not likely that he'll seek you out with an axe in this; it's much more likely that you'll have to sacrifice something very dear to you and give it to him.

It is important also to realize that karma is not the wrath of God but that everyone is the arbiter of his own destiny. Each individual needs to grow up spiritually and to accept that his life is his own responsibility. This is what most orthodox religions miss, for no religion can guarantee you a place in heaven, for heaven or hell is within yourself. Always, actions do, indeed, speak louder than words in your life and action is what karma means. In each today you choose your tomorrow and in the inescapable lessons dealt out by karmic law you will find that they always fit the occasion. If you hate another person in this life then that hatred will come full circle to you in the next. If you enjoy seeing other people suffer then surely your turn will come! Karma is not necessarily immediate although many people have found it to be so in their own lives; it can sometimes take two or three lifetimes for the circle to return to you. Retarded children, mental illness and human tragedy can touch our hearts but, if they are viewed in the light of karmic law, they may be seen in a different light. If you have cruelly dominated others' minds and tried to manipulate and control their destiny, causing them to be the victim, then it is you who will be the victim and be controlled and manipulated in a successive incarnation.

If you can accept that reincarnation is a fact and is working in your life right now alongside karma then you will know that you always have a second chance. If you feel that you can achieve so little in one lifetime or that your talents are not sufficient to do what you desire, then you know that you will get the chance to try again. Acceptance of reincarnation and karma takes away the more painful memories of death, especially when death comes at an early age through an accident or tragedy. Remember that death is a temporary prelude to the spirit entering yet another body – it's a fact not a theory! Science has at last caught up with the fact that reincarnation explains many mysteries and provides plenty of answers to what is happening in everyone's lives. Departments of parapsychology are now attached to schools of medicine, particularly in universities in America, and work done there has resulted in terrific breakthroughs in investigating the memories of ordinary people in every walk of life. Details that they recalled have been minutely investigated and found to be absolutely correct. Books such as *The Bloxham Tapes* and

Who was Bridie Murphy? also substantiate the case for reincarnation, as do the works of Moyra Caldecott and Joan Grant who have remembered their former lives and written them as novels. Yet reading books about other people merely wets the appetite for, by now, curiosity, hopefully, has got the better of you!

If you're asking the questions, 'So who am I?' and 'What has that got to do with my present life?' then read on. There are several methods of remembering past incarnations but you will find that the incarnations you remember are the ones that you need to have knowledge of to help you in your present life. Even if you have been a so-called important person in the past, if this circumstance does not relate to your present life and cannot teach you anything today then this is not the life that you remember. You could remember a fairly humble and lowly one which will prove to be far more important. It is therefore essential if you wish to remember about yourself not to have any preconceived or glamorous ideas of who you were before this life. One of the easiest ways to start is to try to recollect your earliest memories of your childhood. You can do this by talking to parents and grandparents and see if you can fill in the gaps. It is often possible to remember events around the time of birth and simply let the mind wander, latching on to specific incidents as they occur. Many people find that strange things happen when they recollect their earlier childhood memories. You could find yourself in a rather dreamlike state and various pictures could appear, running like a ciné film or even a television picture. If you don't see visually then it's quite possible to sense or feel what has happened around you.

Most remembrances that have been recorded in the last ten years or so have been through hypnosis and although this has resulted in fool-proof evidence, such as the recorded cases in the book *The Bloxham Tapes*, it is not strictly necessary to put yourself in the hands of a hypnotist. Much scientific work has been done with the use of hypnosis and if this is a method you wish to pursue then make quite sure that the hypnotist is a highly ethical and moral character and is fully qualified.

A third method is to catch yourself early in the morning or late at night in that curious state between waking and sleeping. In a drifting, almost mindless, state you often find that energies will appear or that you'll slide back in time into a past life without any effort at all. The trick here is that if you feel or sense anything at all, not to get excited! This is difficult to do but the excitement will stimulate the brain and you will lose your vision. You can, however, train yourself as you gradually wake in the morning to let the mind drift a little longer and see what happens. Many excellent results have been produced this way, but do take care to jot them down as quickly as possible, however fragmentary they may be, for over a period of time they should begin to make sense.

The fourth and best method of all is to find someone who specializes in recall. This is usually a highly developed sensitive or psychic with the ability to create an atmosphere of love and harmony and complete safety. If you work with someone else it is important that you trust them completely or it simply won't work. With a sensitive with experience of the technique of recall, you will simply remember.

'But isn't it all imagination?' I'm often asked. The difference between an imagined life and a real past-life remembrance is quite simple. Once you have remembered a past life it can always return to you, even if you've remembered only a small incident or a part of a day; you can always go back to it in your mind and other parts of other days will come to light. This is never so with imagination for each time it must be conjured anew and is never the same twice. I know because I have experience of this!

Often we form relationships that nobody understands among our family or our friends. These are often karmic relationships. If you have been married in past lives to the same person and the person suddenly appears, the pull will be so great, even though you are apparently happily married already, that you will abandon everything and go with him or her. Alternatively, you could find yourself falling in love at first sight which, in karmic terms, is pure recognition of someone you have known before in another time. This falling in love or recognition can be so strong, no one will prevent you from being together. Often two people get married who are totally dissimilar and seem to have nothing in common, not even love, yet there is some bond that binds them and holds them to each other. Here again it could be the working out of a karmic relationship. You only have to look around you to see this everywhere in daily life. It is indeed a fascinating game!

How do these things affect you now? Remember, karma is concerned with feelings, thoughts and actions. Every thought you have can penetrate somebody's mind and, in fact, can affect the whole environment around you. How many times have you seen an angry person completely change the atmosphere in a room just by being angry! An angry person has an angry house, a peaceful person has a tranquil one and everyone can feel the difference. Your thoughts and your actions can create or destroy all that they touch and your own personal thoughts create an effect that makes karma. In other words, you get what you give, for if you are positive, cheerful and want to give rather than take, you will create and bring conditions which help you find happiness. You do not need to protect yourself from a bully or return anger with anger or distrust with hate. By loving you will create love, not only for yourself but in the world around you.

Edgar Casey did over 14,000 readings with karmic examples of health psychology, family, mental abnormality, etc. For instance, a thirty-eight-year-old woman complained of being unable to commit herself to marriage because of a deep-seated mistrust of men. It turned out that her husband in a previous incarnation had deserted her immediately after their marriage to join the Crusaders. A young homosexual was very unhappy and discovered that he had been in the French Royal Court in his last life and had taken great delight in harassing and exposing homosexuals. Casey said (in trance), 'Condemn not then. What you condemn in another, you will become in yourself.'

Karma comes to you in many different ways and, if you ask for your karma, as I have done, all sorts of things happen most dramatically and traumatically in your life. You may be made aware not only of what you owe other people but that other people owe you. This means allowing them into your life to do whatever they feel is necessary at the time. Remember, you reap what you sow.

Karma can, of course, be applied to animals and many people ask whether man can become an animal or an animal a man over a period of several lives. The answer is that man cannot become an animal despite the beliefs of Egyptians and Hindus. But is it possible, in the evolutionary scale of things, for animals to evolve into super-intelligent animals and then, over a great period of time, evolve into low-level human beings. It is interesting to note, too, that many household pets are often better treated than fellow human beings; perhaps this is karmic payment for having mistreated them in the past! If an animal can eventually evolve into a low-level human being perhaps we should have more compassion for criminals, often regarded as 'animals'. It is also known that the love of a human being speeds up reincarnation for animals, so lavishing all that attention and time on a favourite cat or dog can never be wasted!

It can happen that a pet cat, dog or some other animal comes back to you in a different body. Usually, you know this from your own feelings but a friend of mine has a test which he recommends if you are in doubt. What you do is see in the mind's eye the original pet and then visualize the new one alongside it. Having created them in your mind's eye, try to merge the two images together. If they merge together easily then they are one and the same spirit but, if they remain separate, then the two bodies have different spirits. It's worth a try!

Religion

The basis of all religion is the recognition of a superhuman power that controls our destiny and the belief that there is a personal God who looks after each individual's needs and desires. Yet this definition not only limits what the Creator is all about, but also suggests that you are not responsible for your own thoughts and actions. All the great masters who have shown us the way of truth talk about being part of the Creator, but their main emphasis is on you, yourself, finding truth within your own heart, and discovering for yourself what life and death are all about. Then you can live by spiritual law and understand how things work according to the natural order of things.

You don't have to be a theologian to understand these things. Truth is simple, it is we who insist on making it complicated. Truth is about experiencing love and caring and understanding what it is like to feel clear and free energy inside and outside yourself. So how have we become separated from this idea? How is it that theologians and scholars interpret what the teachers are supposed to have said and done? How is it that religious texts are manipulated and adjusted to suit political or social attitudes? The reason is simple, it takes a brave heart and a great deal of work to look deep inside and accept who and what you are.

If the truth were really known the Churches would lose their power and prestige, and so they developed stories and ideas that created a need for their existence as interpreter and implementer of necessary ceremonies. To confuse everything even more, one religious idea is held to be better than another; so terrible conflicts have been fought in the name of God to 'Save the faith'. All of this ridiculous charade has gone on for centuries with people in authority manipulating the words and acts of the ancient teachings according to their needs and desires. It is not only the authorities who are responsible, because nearly everyone has gone along with it for their own reasons and prejudices.

Now it is about time we all realized that we are *all* seeking the truth and that *all* roads that lead us nearer to this are valid. Gandhi said, 'Religions are different roads converging on the same point. What does it matter that we take different roads so long as we reach the same goal.' This is exactly what searching for truth is all about. Gandhi also saw that the form of the House of God was not important, it was what went on *inside* that house that meant something. He said:

Bitter experience has taught me that all temples are not houses of God . . . they can be temptations of the Devil. These places have no value unless the keeper is a man of God. Temples, mosques, and churches are what man makes them to be.

Religion tends to teach religion and not spirituality. God assumes the role of the Creator and controller, while spirituality teaches that an individual is a co-creator with God, and part of God. It is this aspect which is ignored a great deal in some religions. You are responsible for your own behaviour, your own life, and what you experience. The great teachers can point you in the right direction, but it is up to you whether you accept or take up the challenges of life and how much knowledge and wisdom you gain. This is not to say that all who follow religion are wasting their time, because many just and noble people have worked to spread the truth through religious practices. But it is very sad to see the authorities still keeping up pretences that stop people from finding the truth. The Christian Church, for example, used to teach the idea of reincarnation, and yet now it denies its existence. By doing so, it changes the whole perspective of spiritual development. There are many other theological points that make it much harder to penetrate the truth of things and they create obscure and useless dogma.

It is a tragedy that religion for us means today nothing more than restriction on food and drink; nothing more than adherence to a sense of superiority and inferiority. There cannot be a grosser ignorance than this.

Mahatma Gandhi

All you can do, whether you follow a religious idea or not, is look inside your own heart, try to find your inner peace and truth, and listen to your inner voice. You can always tell whether it is truth or not because things ring with the sound of truth and they *feel* right. You cannot learn through the intellect, but you can experience truth inside your inner heart and mind. It is the inner knowing that should be encouraged and developed so that you really do know what is going on inside yourself. If you take responsibility for yourself and work towards making yourself clearer and more aware, then you will not only be much happier but you won't have the dreadful threat of the Devil, hell and judgement over your head. As Frances Bacon said, 'A little philosophy inclineth men's minds to atheism, but depth of philosophy bringeth men's minds about to religion.'

Blind faith is our greatest enemy and stops us from finding something inside ourselves that is very real and very worthwhile. Inner religion is the best way to proceed with things and if this can be integrated into an exterior religious idea as well, then that is fine. Religion has evolved because great masters have come to the earth and shown us how to find truth. It is us who have distorted these teachings, creating dogma and ridiculous rules that do not relate to everyday life. As the *Bhagavad-Gita* states:

One who restrains the senses and organs of action, but whose mind dwells on sense objects, certainly deludes and is called a pretender. On the other hand, he who controls the senses by the mind and engages his active organs in works of devotion, without attachment, is by far superior.

Runes

Few people had heard of runes even ten years ago, but now more and more people are telling fortunes using this ancient European method. This is one of the simplest

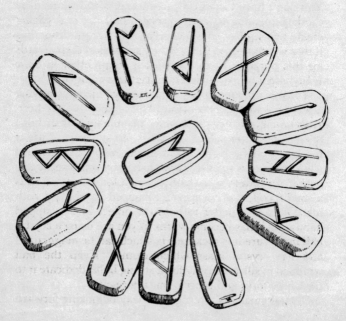

forms of practical magic. Runes are usually small objects of stone, wood or ceramic with hieroglyphics engraved on them. The runic letters themselves carry the power and energies are invoked during the working. Most people work with twenty-four runes, plus one to represent fate or karma. In the past, the Vikings were most attached to runic invocation; many objects and artefacts from that time are engraved with runescripts. Runes can be used in a constructive and helpful way in many areas of life, such as protective devices, healing, concentration or making the path of love go smoothly. If you enjoy magic, runes seem a simplistic way and a non-harmful one.

Scrying or Crystal Gazing

You don't have to wear a turban and be surrounded by exotic furnishing to read a crystal ball. Crystal gazing create this state of consciousness. An Arab tradition has it that warriors used the polished surfaces of their swords for this purpose. Even the wicked step-mother in *Snow White* used a mirror to find out what was going on.

You can use almost any small, shiny object for scrying although a rock-quartz crystal ball is probably the best. It is possible to use a tumbler or small goldfish bowl filled with water while, in Tibet, crystal gazers use a black crystalline stone found in the mountain streams; while gazing, its surface is kept bright by splashing water over it. In India the usual equivalent for a crystal ball is a small bowl, saucer or even a cupped hand filled with ink. Often it is better to hold the object in the cupped hand until it has become warm. If you are using a crystal ball make sure it is rock-quartz which can be magnetized and not crystal glass which cannot. Keep the ball wrapped in silk and away from strong light, dedicate it to the Christ force and programme it for truth.

Crystal gazing is a recognized way of looking forward

into the future, but it can also be used to see into the past.

Start by being physically comfortable and relaxed. Put your crystal on a cushion of black velvet, dim the lights and gaze intently at it. You may need to meditate, relax and to keep your emotions as quiet as possible. A relaxed state of mind and body is the key. Your attitude is very important so keep an open mind above all things. The first thing that happens is that the crystal will go out of focus and you won't be able to see its outline very well. It will then jump back in detail and then out of focus again. You could also experience a tight band around the forehead as if someone has put a metal helmet on you that is one size too small. Don't be discouraged if this seems to have derived from even more ancient ways of looking at the haunting quality of reflected images. The ancient Greeks used a calm surface of water and, later on, a mirror as a means of entering a trance which enabled them to see the future. Any reflective surface can happens for it means that your psychic abilities are developing. The surface of the crystal could cloud over and become misty or you could even see sparks of light. When this happens, be still and wait. Pictures can come but they tend to be fragmentary. It is rather like dreaming as you will get faces and colours or even symbols. If you keep your mind poised but relaxed and don't get excited you'll do well, otherwise you will lose the vision. If you tend to get symbols then learn what the symbolic forms mean to you. For instance, a pyramid could mean ancient Egypt to one person and the eternal triangle to another! Train yourself to understand the symbols your inner senses present to you.

If you wish to go back into the past, picture time as a road of living memory which starts from yourself and ends within the heart of the crystal. As you concentrate and gaze more and more you'll feel a link beginning to grow between the crystal and yourself. This will reach deeper and deeper through the conscious into the subconscious mind. By this time you could be feeling rather dreamy and vague and that is exactly how you should be. Start by concentrating on yesterday or even last week or last year and slowly regress to early childhood. If you want to go into a past life you can do this also, allowing things to come naturally and gently. Everything must proceed at its own pace. Don't try to hurry or push or the vision will end. When you have finished the session the most important thing is to shut off and close yourself down.

It is usually best to simply announce that the session is finished and say so out loud. Do this calmly, with determination. It is often a good idea to have something to eat or do some physical activity. Remember, that being a good clairvoyant means not only unfolding your own power but learning how to control it. It is a great responsibility if you are reading for someone else; so ask yourself if you really want this responsibility before you become an oracle.

Seances

At the turn of the century, seances were almost parlour entertainment and there was plenty of table tapping and table turning. A real seance, though, consists of a group of people who want to contact the spirits of the dead. A trained medium should be present to guard the group against all the mischievous and dangerous energies and to allow proper contact to be established. The amateur type of seance is usually done for 'fun'. This involves a Ouija board or a glass that moves around spelling out the answers. The first one that I ever took part in was after a party when I was quite young. It was uncanny when the glass moved for it certainly worked even though we hadn't a clue what was going on. Now I am wiser and know that, unless there is someone who is trained and disciplined, you will not get into the right space and could tap into some murky energies which are quite real and very dangerous. Sitting in a group does create a powerful energy which can be used constructively by a trained person but creates a disturbance when it is not channelled properly. If you do want to do this sort of thing, contact someone who is trained in this area so at least you'll be safe if anything goes wrong.

Sneezing

The sneeze has played an important part in folklore and can either be seen as a good or bad omen. The sneeze can represent the spirit of life, as it did in Aristotle's time, when the first sign of the recovery of a patient who was thought to be dying was a sneeze. In European folklore a sick person who sneezed could look forward to the restoration of his full health in the near future. The sneeze has also been seen as a bad omen and symbolized the expulsion of life from the body. According to an American superstition, sneezing at a meal is a sign of death in the family! A sneeze was also the sign of a psychic attack or possession, for it was thought that demons might enter the body through the nostrils; so in some cultures they were protected by amulets or sometimes nose rings. Scottish superstition states that a baby remains under the control of the fairies until its first sneeze. The act of sneezing nowadays usually takes the form of a blessing. The English say 'Bless you.' The Zulu says 'I am now blessed.' The Hindu says 'live' and his friends say 'with you'. The Romans used to say 'Banish the omen' after someone sneezed, while Aristotle mentions a similar custom among the Greeks.

The custom of saying 'God bless you' after sneezing was started by Pope Gregory the Great in the sixth century, during the outbreak of a plague in Rome. The nursery rhyme, 'Ring a Ring of Roses' is a reference to the Great Plague and 'atishoo, atishoo, we all fall down' refers to the sneeze which was a fatal symptom of the Plague.

Even today, the sneeze is still seen as an omen. It is not a good omen to sneeze on New Year's Eve; if you do you should visit three homes before midnight to offset the curse. In Europe three sneezes indicate the presence of four thieves, while in Finland if two pregnant women sneeze simultaneously then they look forward to twins. The Japanese believe that to sneeze once means a blessing, twice you are guilty and thrice you will be ill; so, when you have your next cold, make sure you only have single sneezes!

Soul and Soul Mates

What is a man profitted, if he shall gain the whole world, and lose his own soul?

Matthew 16:26

The soul is the clothing around the spirit, the supple yet firm barrier between the pure spirit inside and the physical world on the outside. The soul acts as a filter and a communication centre between spirit and matter. It absorbs and sorts out all the experiences of the physical, mental and spiritual worlds, so that the pure spirit inside can absorb the essence of the experience without receiving the rubbish. The soul is a communication centre looking after all your needs so that your inner spirit can gain knowledge and wisdom. The soul body is usually most active when you're asleep or in a relaxed state, as it tends to use the unconscious mind to plant ideas and changes that the internal spirit deems necessary. It is possible to have direct communication with other spirits and souls or the universal soul, but you do need to be asleep or spiritually advanced to do this at will. The soul is not physical although it does look after all the physical needs of the body and directs the whole of the body's functions via the brain. As the spirit is housed in dense, physical matter, the soul makes sure that the physical body is in the best condition to evolve itself into a higher vibration, in order that the spirit can function in a clearer and more efficient way through the physical shell.

The idea of a soul or the universal spirit is mentioned in many ancient teachings. They describe a vast ocean of light and spirit that gradually changes from the passive role to an active role. This started to break up the unity and wholeness, forming portions of spirit that still vibrated at the same rate but were distinctly separate. One portion of this is called mankind and it continued to split again and again, forming millions of parts. As the portions divided, they formed vessels so the universal spirit could be kept pure; these are known as the soul vessels. Gradually, these descended into dense physical matter, so that the universal spirit could experience absolute separation. Although the breaking down caused separation, it did not break up the vibration deep inside every individual so that connections and ties were maintained. The parts of the universal spirit that are close to you are called your soul group; as this group broke down it formed several individuals, known as your soul mates. You may have come across many of these in your family, friends or loved ones, now or in your previous incarnations. The final split was quite a unique division for you personally, because it was like dividing a circle which can only be reformed by both sides coming together again. Half of it is you, the other half is your soul partner. It is the desire deep within that pushes you on to find your soul partner so that you can return to a feeling of wholeness, experiencing truth and obtaining a sense of being at one with yourself. Both halves compliment each other, your strengths and weaknesses support and balance each other. Your fears are your partner's experiences, his fears are your experiences. You fit together like a dovetail joint. To accomplish this demands the hardest test of all for you have to overcome all your conflicts, fears and illusions and he has to do the same. You vibrate at exactly the same electromagnetic frequency so both sides have to match or there will be quite an explosion.

As you can imagine, it is very rare that soul partners meet on every level but, when they do, it sounds a vibration right the way through the whole of creation because it strikes a new note in the cosmic order; so keep on looking because, one day, you will accomplish one of the most difficult tasks in the universe, to experience total separation and isolation, and total unity and harmony, in a conscious manner. When you do this you help your soul family, the soul group, and your soul partner to move nearer to the whole again.

Speaking in Tongues

This was implemented long before Christianity, but it is probably best known because of that, for the Apostles had to teach in many different languages and countries. There were not the educational and intellectual facilities available to allow them to learn twenty or thirty languages. By opening themselves to the will of the Creator, it became possible to speak in many dialects with great ease. In this way the teachings could come through with great energy and the people listening to them understood completely. Gradually this form has been misunderstood and tends to be misused; a great many people can speak in tongues but they are of no use to anyone.

A dear friend of mine from Findhorn has the ability to speak in tongues. This is not uncommon. When my friend went into trance and his guide came through, he spoke in a language that neither my friend nor I knew. We didn't even know the name of the language. After talking for about twenty minutes, I plucked up the courage to talk to the guide myself and suggested that, if he learnt English, everyone would be able to appreciate the message he was bringing through. So he did! Although I appreciated my friend's channelling, it didn't seem to be much use if you didn't understand, although he assured me that I was absorbing it at a high level; nevertheless, I certainly couldn't have passed the message on to anyone else.

Speaking in tongues is the activity of tapping into collective energies over the centuries and gradually being able to talk in various languages of great antiquity. Today, man's intellect has progressed a great deal and we are capable of learning a great many languages in a short amount of time. There are now great teachers available who have developed spiritually and, therefore, there is a wider availability of people doing brotherhood work. If the person speaking in foreign languages and in strange dialects and tongues could go into their own space when they are doing it, they would discover that they either lived in the place they were speaking from or that they were teachers that went all over the country in early Christian times. Today, they need to change gear and come up to the present time, so that they will be able to teach great things in the language of the country they are living in now.

Spirit Guide

Everyone has a spirit guide, or doorkeeper, whose job it is to make sure that you complete your task on the earth and learn the lessons that you had agreed to learn before you incarnated. Being a spirit guide or doorkeeper is a very frustrating business for few of us give them the time or space to communicate properly. Perhaps in dreams, or in that time between waking and sleeping which I call the twilight zone, your guide can get messages to you.

Meditation is by far the best method to make contact and this needs to be carefully done with an expert.

As the doorkeeper or spirit guide's whole job is looking after you, and making sure you meet the people that you are meant to meet, and helping to set up the situations that you're meant to go into, making communication with them consciously speeds everything up. I can't imagine life without this contact as I chat to my guides regularly during the day about all sorts of things. Your guide is linked to you by love and by nothing else, for it is not the case of the guide being assigned to you. Indeed not. They have known you through several lives and you have probably worked together in a very close relationship at some time or another. It is through love that they are with you and through love that they help you achieve all you have agreed to do. A guide can never push or manipulate for you're not a puppet. They can only guide and advise if they are asked, and be a companion to you. Most people never know their spirit guide consciously at all and they live and work and die in ignorance of the wonderful companionship and love that can exist. Today, with more awareness and understanding, more and more people are seeking to know their spirit guide, and I do a great deal of work with meditation techniques so that this can come about. It never fails!

Often you have more than one guide for, although the doorkeeper has been with you since you first drew breath as a little baby, other guides will come in from time to time simply because they are interested in the work that you're doing, or hope to do. If you're a doctor or studying medicine, it is quite likely that doctors or healers will come and give you a hand. Some stay for a short while, while others stay for many years. If you write books then those who are interested in your literary achievements will certainly be there to help and, perhaps at the same time, to complete something that they felt was unfinished during their time on earth.

Spiritualism

Spiritualism has always been with us for it is simply the belief that, after death, you continue in a non-physical existence. It is this communication between those who have died and those who are still on planet earth, that is the foundation of spiritualism. The spiritualist medium is the person who links the two worlds and is the spirit communicator.

Spiritualism is also a religion and dates from the mid-nineteenth century with the mediumship of the Fox sisters, in the United States of America. It all started with table tapping and, overnight, spiritualism exploded into the public eye, complete with practitioners and followers. Every small town had its medium and everyone was anxious to converse with spirits throughout the length and breadth of the land. After about fifty years everything calmed down though, even today, spiritualism provides wonderful solace and consolation for those who are bereaved and wish to communicate with loved ones. There was, of course, much fraudulence as well as genuine communication, and psychic research came into its own. At that time, a typical seance could be quite spectacular. Disembodied hands waved about, an accordian could start up with no fingers visibly playing it, and a medium's body could change shape and dimension. Often a simple cone-shaped trumpet, floating in a darkened room, was used for the spirit voice to go through. Some mediums could materialize apports such as jewels and flowers supposed to be gifts from the spirits, while others simply went into trance.

Modern spiritualism is defined by spiritualists as 'a religion because it strives to understand and to comply with the physical, mental and spiritual laws of nature which are the laws of God'. Besides communicating with spirits of the dead as proof of survival, the spiritualist church does a great deal of work with healing. The spiritualist minister is able to perform marriages and services and the mediums have to reach a certain standard in order to be able to perform.

One thing that is never, ever emphasized by the mediums, however, is that you can do it all yourself. Many people continue to go to mediums for comfort and guidance but it is very rarely suggested that you can do this yourself and that your own guidance is always the best. There is no attempt at all to put this across and to ask you what you *feel* about a situation. All too often they act as Mr Fixit. Yet, in fact, nothing is fixed at all.

Spiritual Law

Spiritual law is not the ten commandments or any other set of words that are deemed to be the word of God. The law is a series of observations on the way things work in a spiritual and physical universe. The word 'spiritual' denotes the idea of the life force that penetrates everything that is spiritual, mental, emotional or physical. The Chinese describe the law as the Tao, the way of things, the cosmic process in which everything is seen as a continuous flow of expansion and contraction; this flow is called change. The Chinese made observations and saw that, when a situation develops to its extreme, it naturally turns round and becomes its opposite. If a person wants to travel East he will eventually land up in the West, and if you become rich you will eventually become poor. This is the way of things and was seen to be the interplay between the opposites, although a pair of opposites was also seen as a unity – the conscious and the unconscious are a pair of opposites. The movements of the Tao, or the Way, are not a force that is exerted on to something, but occur naturally and spontaneously. A Chinese sage once stated, 'Those who follow the natural order, flow in the current of the Tao.'

Spiritual law is a practical guide to how things change, why they change in a particular way and what that change will bring about, depending on whether you are flowing spontaneously with the situation or resisting the flow of change. The existence of spiritual law has only come about because the wisest of mankind have studied the way things work and have assimilated this knowledge into teachings. This knowledge is a way of expanding the consciousness of mankind and may be 'universal kind', and is the basis for all the religious and mystical ideas in the world today. You will not be able to find spiritual laws written down in a single form, you can only find examples of how they work by looking at things yourself, examining why things happen inside and outside yourself, and seeing whether you are flowing spontaneously or not. Look into physical life and beyond it so that you can get a wider perspective of how and why things work according to their own natural patterns.

An example of much spiritual law can be examined if we take a look at a person who is selfish. This will apply whether they are on the earth, in another galaxy or in spirit, because they will all have one thing in common. They all restrict their full potential because they box themselves into a smaller and smaller space by trying to cling on to the things they believe are theirs. Sooner or later, they will experience a restriction which will begin to suffocate them. After a while they will lose everything and experience suffering. Eventually, though, they will see the cause of their suffering and will let go of all they are holding on to. Immediately they do this, as a mental or physical act, they will find that the things they need will stay with them and the things they have been wanting will only go away from them if it is necessary. A natural spontaneous balance will be struck. From that moment on, the consciousness of the person will understand that particular flow of things, absorbing the knowledge of spiritual law by direct experience. This is not to say that the person will understand every aspect of this law but that they will be able to see its different manifestations much more easily in the future.

This type of situation is not new and will continue. The situation also existed thousands of years ago and was seen to occur again and again. When analysed it was seen that the cause was a lack of understanding and a resistance to the natural flow of things. This had an effect, an inability to cope with sharing and change; the result was suffering because the individual could not flow. This suffering is referred to as karma, the idea that every activity puts you more out of synchronicity with the natural patterns (therefore you experience suffering), or it keeps you in line with the flows (therefore you experience happiness). This balancing act can span many lifetimes and it is thought that your present life conditions are a result of your past actions, while your present actions will determine your future conditions. This is also part of the natural flow of change and part of spiritual law.

The laws that can be seen to affect a human situation can also be applied in universal terms. A series of particles gradually came together and an intense heat and pressure formed together over thousands of years. This act was a spontaneous flow of creation. When it came to a certain point it exploded to form galaxies, solar systems and planets. This expansion will eventually reach a point where the opposite will start to take place. This is not a punishment but a natural flow.

Everything that exists flows with life force and that force can never stay still; therefore, the idea of change occurs. Everything we do, our planet does and the galaxy does, affects everything else, and everything else affects us to some degree or other. Everything, therefore, can be seen as adhering to the law or resisting the law. Happiness, according to the Taoists, is achieved when we follow the natural order, acting spontaneously, trusting our intuitive knowledge. By doing this, our consciousness expands so that we can be at one with ourselves and the idea of God. This is described by an ancient Chinese Sage, called Chuang Tsu, in his book of the same name. The men of old shared the placid tranquillity which belonged to the whole world. At that time the Yin and Yang were harmonious and still; their resting and moving proceeded without any disturbance; the four seasons had their definitive times; not a single thing received any injury and no living being came to a premature end. Men might be possessed of the faculty of knowledge, but they had no occasion for its use. This is what is called the State of Perfect Unity. At this time there was no action on the part of anyone, but a constant manifestation of spontaneity.

Spontaneous Human Combustion

Spontaneous human combustion is the consumption of the human body by intense heat, with no apparent outside causes. There have been many reports of this happening over the years with no conclusive evidence to suggest the causes. In the John Dentley case of 1966 only the bottom half of his leg was found in his bathroom, the floor was burnt right through but nothing else was damaged. In July 1951 Mary Reeser was found in St Petersburg, Florida. Sha had died in her armchair which was also destroyed in the fire. There was a blackened circle, no more than a metre in diameter, and all that could be seen was a few springs and the metal frame-work of her lamp. All that remained of her was one foot, a small piece of backbone, and her skull, shrunk to the size of an orange. A world-famous forensic scientist stated that this never happens to skulls exposed to normal radiation of intense heat; they either become swollen or break into pieces. Theoretically, bones should have been visible as calcined fragments even after twelve hours of continous heat of 3000°F. In 1922 the calcined bones of Mrs Johnson, a sixty-eight-year-old widow living in Sydenham, were found; her clothes were undamaged. Another case describes Mrs Carpenter who was on a boat on holiday on the Norfolk Broads; suddenly, she burst into flames and was reduced to ashes in front of her husband and children.

This phenomenon happens very seldom, and is unpredictable; recently, it has been suggested that the earth's magnetic disturbances seem to occur in the area at the same time. Any writers of the subject have drawn a parallel with poltergeist behaviour in the way fire appears suddenly, as if from another dimension. Whatever the reasons for such happenings, they have irrational elements that will be hard to contain within an orthodox framework of science.

Charles Dickens was fascinated with this gothic horror, as it was called in the nineteenth century. He wrote about it at length in *Bleak House* (chapter 32). Here the evil crook is mysteriously burnt to ashes and, as Dickens explains, 'call the death by any name, attribute it to whom you will . . . engendered in the corrupt humours of the vicious body itself and that only, spontaneous combustion and none other of all the deaths that can be died'.

Superstition

Superstition is all a state of mind, yet it affects everybody at some level or other. Do you cross your fingers or always throw a pinch of salt over your left shoulder when you spill some? Or perhaps you consider a black cat to be lucky?

Good or bad luck has always been tied up with superstition and, however logical, rational or full of commonsense you may be you will probably find yourself doing some of these things.

You have probably noticed that some people are invariably lucky while others leave behind them a trail of bad luck. If you believe you are lucky, you probably will be and if you believe that a certain lucky charm, ring or colour is good for you, then it probably will be. The psychologist Jung called this synchronicity and said that the person's individual psychological state attracts certain specific events. In other words, if you feel lucky you have a greater chance of being lucky; the reverse is equally true! As a result you have probably been brought up not to put up umbrellas in the house, or bring a sprig of may into the house. Touch wood is one that works for most of us, that is if we can find anything wooden in this age of plastic and synthetics. If you accept the existence of forces beyond those appreciated by the five physical senses, there is every reason to believe it does work for, in principle, touching wood is like earthing an electrical appliance. It is quite possible that, if it works on one level, it may work on another.

Superstition is very strong among actors and actresses and it is considered bad luck to wear real flowers on the stage, to say the last word of a play before the final rehearsal or to wear green. To wish an actor or a play good luck on the first night is supposed to mean disaster and no one will venture into a dressing-room numbered thirteen.

Thirteen is considered unlucky by most, particularly Friday the thirteenth – not to me, however, as that was the day I was born.

As I have said, it is all in the mind! It is seldom that you find a thirteenth floor in a skyscraper or a hotel room numbered thirteen, even today. Sportsmen go to great lengths to be lucky and carry sprigs of white heather, sentimental coins and even certain caps or hats which they regard as lucky. A lucky putter for a golfer or a lucky tennis racquet or cricket ball are all important. A German proverb says, 'Luck follows the hopeful, ill luck the fearful', so the answer is obviously in your own mind.

Table Turning

Around the 1850s in the long, dark, winter evenings it was almost a fashionable pastime for the Victorians to practise table turning. It was a form of attempted communication with spirits and was rather similar to the use of the Ouija board. Several people would seat themselves round a table with their hands lightly spread on the surface and their fingers touching those of their companions to the left and right. The lights were then lowered and the table would rock slightly and, by an agreed code, spell out messages. It would also bump on the floor and any rapping noises would be interpreted as answers. Most codes were simply a tap for 'Yes' and two for 'No'. This method is rarely used today and, although I have a friend Aline who gets raps and taps we have become far more sophisticated. Like automatic writing, the Ouija and planchette methods, it lends itself all too readily to subconscious motivation. In the past, table turning would result in the table rising into the air or even being forcibly hurled across a room. This activity can also involve poltergeists and can be quite dangerous. After all, the table has to land somewhere!

Tai Chi Cho'an

Tai Chi Cho'an is meditating in movement. The movements eventually become one complete movement that helps you to feel and use the natural energies within yourself and the earth. The movements are called the form and there are many different styles although they work on the same principle: to use the energies that are within and without. Though approaching this in a physical way you can touch the deeper mysteries through thought, feeling and action. You should be able to increase your Chi energy in order to prevent attack upon yourself or, if you are attacked, to yield in such a way that the person who is attacking you has nothing to hook his aggression onto. The ultimate idea of self-defence is to be so harmonious as to never bring the conditions that lead to a violent situation towards you. Tai Chi is a way to understand how to bring this about.

Tarot

Tarot cards have their roots in the antiquity of occultism and have always been used for foretelling the future. Priests of the late Egyptian empire realized that their successors in each generation were becoming less worthy to continue their religious teachings. They resorted to the simple but wise way of ensuring the survival of their knowledge by reducing their scripture to a set of symbols and incorporating these into a pack of seventy-eight cards which could be used for both gambling and fortune telling. These cards became the tarot. The gypsies carried the pack as well. Today, anyone can read the tarot who has the eyes to see and the heart to understand.

Tarot is the gypsies' bible. You can trace the tarot's origin to the gypsies who wandered from India into Europe, for the cards' markings distilled all Egyptian knowledge.

Little is known about the development of the tarot pack. The minor arcana, face and number cards from which modern playing cards derive, seem to represent not only kings, queens and knaves, but also peasants, symbolized by the wand, clergy, by the cup, nobles, by the sword, and merchants, by the coins. It was felt in the nineteenth century that there was prophetic power in the symbols: the wand foretold news; the cup happiness and contentment; the sword death and the coin money.

The intuition and interpretation of the practitioner is what counts, however. Divining by tarot cards is as individual as crystal gazing or any other form of fortune

THE LOVERS

telling. There is not one single authoritative book of
instruction, although numerous volumes on technique
have been published. Personality, attitude and inclina-
tion of whoever reads the cards are all-important. As
with any other method, an altered state of consciousness
seems to be valuable to interpretation. Tarot cards differ
from playing cards in that their upper and lower halves
have different values. Pictures that are placed right side
up have one meaning; placed face down the meaning is
reversed.

With tarot reading, you will be asked to shuffle the
cards; this is done so that your personal vibration is
transmitted to them. You might be asked to cut the cards
and may even need to shuffle them again. Tarot cards
are usually wrapped in silk or cloth before they are used.
A tarot reader will lay out the cards in a particular
formation, two of the most popular being a twelve-card

spread, (two rows of six cards), or a formation of a pyramid known as the Bohemian spread. Other methods are the mystical cross, the magic square (three rows of three cards) and the Horoscope spread (the cards laid out in the twelve houses like a birth chart). How the cards are laid out doesn't matter so much as the way that they are interpreted. The symbolic figures on the cards represent the stages in Man's destiny. They are divided into a major arcana of twenty-two cards and a minor arcana of fifty-six cards. In the minor arcana are four suites: cups, swords, pentacles and sceptres. There are fourteen in each suite. The major arcana presents deep esoteric insight, demanding close study and concentration; here ESP ability is so invaluable.   Tarot readings are often given in conjunction with crystal readings or palmistry.

Telepathy

Telepathy is the communication of thoughts and images from one mind to another; thought is creative and can be shifted about from place to place. The word 'telepathy' comes from two Greek words which, together, mean 'feeling at a distance'. Most people have telepathic communications during an average week. How many times, for instance, have you thought about telephoning someone only to discover that that person is telephoning you, or have written a letter that's long overdue to someone who has written to you at the same time. You don't have to be trained in order to be telepathic for there is plenty of communication between average families. If you want to try to train yourself to be more receptive or to give out telepathic signals it's quite possible to do this. Being calm and patient is a great help and it doesn't work unless there is some emotional charge in the message you wish to send. To be successful make sure the message you want to send is as short as it possibly can be and then send either a highly charged signal or a flashing signal rather like the beam of light a lighthouse sends out every few seconds. It's also possible for a group of people to transmit a combined message to a single person, and vice versa. This all operates in the subconscious levels of the minds of both the sender and the receiver; all the sender has to do is to form a very clear picture of the thought to be sent, together with the emotion connected with it. Obviously, being able to visualize clearly is very important and you can train yourself to do this over a period of time. Just think how much money you'd save in telephone bills!

Third Eye

This is said to be placed between the eyebrows and connected in some way to the pineal gland in the mid-brain area. The third eye is said to have seven veils of protection though it may have twelve. As you become psychically more developed the veils slowly dissolve until the eye is fully open. With training you will be able to open and shut the eye as you need to perceive. People think claivoyants walk along the streets and travel on the trains with the eye open but this is not the case. We simply couldn't live with that. The third eye is deliberately opened when the need arises and then closed again.

Trance and Trance Mediums

In the past a mediumistic trance was a rather sleeplike condition which allowed the medium's body to be used by a discarnate spirit. Today, however, being a trance medium doesn't mean that you go to sleep and don't remember what you are doing; though this is a self-induced state, I, and many of my friends, remember exactly what is said and expressed. The approach to a mediumistic trance is also quite different to the way it used to be. Before there were many deep breaths; now you simply sit and allow it to happen, although relaxation helps and training is essential. The way I teach people is to sit comfortably in a chair and imagine the spine is very fluid; so fluid that it simply merges into the back of the chair and you have a sensation of falling backwards, though knowing you are completely safe and completely protected. The most difficult thing with training a medium to speak is to get them started, so whatever words come into your head, just have the courage to repeat them out loud. The first sentence will be followed by the second, and then the third and fourth quite rapidly. As your confidence grows, then your spirit guide can become closer and closer to you, eventually making your normal voice more like their voice and your face more like their face. Depth of trance depends very much on your spiritual state, and also the power and energy of the spirit guide. It is really a wonderful feeling. I always feel a tremendous sense of honour being able to do this work. A medium really is a telephone line, and the clearer the line the clearer the communication. You need to work very hard on yourself to be able to achieve the clarity that is required, but it is well worth it. Sometimes, I feel I am standing behind myself when I am in a trance. At other times I seem to expand and go off to a garden somewhere, while other times I am simply beyond the earth itself, feeling completely part of everything and everything part of me. It is quite normal for the guide to use his own mannerisms and gestures, as well as his own peculiar ways of phraseology and words. Perhaps the most impressive thing of all is the tremendous amount of love that comes through and the great desire to encourage and inspire. It took me a long time to become a trance medium: seven years. I would sit in a development circle with a very dear, older friend and my doorkeeper or spirit guide would practice an exercise of standing behind me and asking me to imagine falling backwards into his arms. We did this every Wednesday night, week in and week out, for seven years, until one day I thought 'Here we go again'! I fell backwards and he wasn't there but was standing in front of me. I then realized that I had released my control and was able to channel. It is this release of the spine and will that enables you to become the human telephone line. It is also being able to trust and to know that the love from the spirit guide is so strong that no harm can come to you. I certainly know that is true.

Unconscious Mind

In Freud's view the unconscious mind was a place where painful memories are held in a repressed state. Jung called these repressed thoughts and feelings 'the personal unconscious' and went on to suggest the idea of a 'collective unconscious' which contained all man's memories and experiences. Jung felt that the unconscious mind is not only a shadow of the past, but also provides a pool of information that can be dipped into to help sort out the future. Most of the investigations of the unconscious mind have been through dream interpretation, because dreams are seen as the 'language of the unconscious'.

During hypnosis facts and detailed knowledge of subjects unknown to the conscious mind are remembered; this is not so surprising because it is thought that the unconscious mind records everything in the external world faster and more accurately than the conscious mind and the information is retained totally. Through hypnosis and mind-relaxation techniques the barrier between the conscious and unconscious mind is removed and the information is released. You can do this yourself by developing a controlled and relaxed conscious mind, allowing the unconscious mind to have a bigger influence on decision-making. Meditation, contemplation and relaxation are all ways to reduce the activity of the conscious mind so that the intuitive, sometimes called the unconscious, mind, can come forward and provide solutions, wisdom and foresight, unrevealed in the turmoil of the conscious mind.

Unidentified Flying Objects (UFOs)

There are records of UFOs from as long ago as 2000BC, although the term 'Flying Saucer' was coined in 1947 by an American who saw disc-shaped objects over Washington and said that they were 'flying like a saucer would if it skimmed over water'.

There are thousands of reports of UFOs every year and, although some of them are fakes, there is enough evidence to suggest that they do exist. There were many rumours in the 1940s of a UFO that was reported to have crashed; it was said that the occupants and their ship were taken by US officials in total secrecy. The idea that extra-terrestials have landed may seem far-fetched but reports of this increase every year. In the 1950s, Howard Menger claimed he had met people from other planets and that they gave him a guided tour of the solar system. Another case shows a photograph of a dead pilot of a UFO which came down near Mexico City in the late fifties. The body of the pilot was 'lost' on its way to Germany for examination.

In 1964 a police patrolman saw a bluish-orange flame in the sky that descended some distance away. He gave chase and eventually came across a shining aluminium object, 200 yards below him, which looked like a car tilted on its end. He then saw two humanoid figures in white overalls, two metres tall, close to the object. One of them turned around, saw him and seemed to jump. The patrolman started going towards them thinking they might need help.

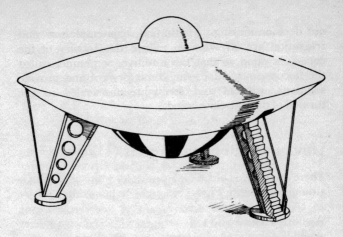

The terrain became too rough for the car and so he proceeded on foot. He left the car and heard three loud thumps, like the slamming of a door. When he was about fifty paces from the object there was a loud roar which became louder and louder. He saw the same bluish-orange flame that he had seen before and the object rose from the ground, leaving a cloud of dust. The patrolman made a hasty retreat, seeing the oval shape, now horizontal, rising into the sky. When his sergeant arrived they investigated the fire that was still burning and found four separate burn marks and four depressions which they assumed were from the legs of the landing gear.

Some people have claimed that they were abducted by aliens and, surprisingly, the descriptions are all similar. The aliens are said to be of small stature, of childlike appearance, with large eyes and slit-like mouths. Two drawings were made during separate incidents, reported independently. Perhaps the film 'Close Encounters of the Third Kind' got it right after all.

Close encounters of the third kind, that is, where UFO occupants are observed, occur quite often. The pattern is always the same. The craft is silent and suddenly disappears; while watching it the observers feel paralysed and unable to speak. There is a definite time distortion. Whereas they may think that five minutes has transpired, it more likely to be an hour or two.

UFO occupants are generally said to communicate by telepathy and UFOs are often associated with poltergeist activities.

My husband has had a couple of direct experiences with UFOs. Several years ago he was piloting a Cessna plane between Los Angeles and Las Vegas over the Mojave Desert in California. He was flying at around 14,000 feet, a broken cloud layer above him, when he saw something, looking like a weather balloon, that simply appeared and disappeared again. A few seconds later two large silver discs flew under the plane along the desert floor at a tremendously fast speed. He knew they were metallic as they looked like aluminium and glinted in the sun. He thought they were about a hundred feet in diameter and had a convex shape. They were both flying together and so fast that he turned to his co-pilot and, before he could say anything, they had gone. The whole incident lasted about fifteen seconds.

The other incident occurred a few years later when he was flying over Albuquerque, New Mexico, at around 11 p.m. at 12,000 feet in another Cessna plane. His co-pilot pointed out a huge green fireball directly in line with the flight path, slightly above them. It was so bright that it lit up the cockpit and they were both stunned and surprised at the same time.

Utopia

In 1516 Thomas More published a book called *Utopia* which talked of an imaginary island governed by a perfect political and social system. In 1933 a novel called *Lost Horizon* was published; this told of two pilots lost in the Himalayas who found a community cut off from the world. It described a society where life was run according to the collective wisdom of ancient arts and sciences. Its adepts lived in peace and harmony, doing as they thought fit, guided a little by the past but still more by their present wisdom and by their clairvoyance of the future. This place was called Shangri-La and many people believe such a place exists. Another novel was based on a Far Eastern legend of a hidden paradise lying in Tibet or Mongolia. This place is called Chang Shambhala 'a Northern Place of Quietude'. There are several other similar traditions in India, China, Russia and Tibet. They all talk of the most wise and knowledgeable of men living in seclusion in inaccessible parts of Asia. The idea is also reiterated by historians and philosophers in Greece and Rome and even Pythagoras was reputed to have travelled to Hindustan to seek it. Shambhala, itself, is supposed to be in Tibet in an enclosed valley where hot springs nourish the rich vegetation and many rare plants and medicinal herbs are able to grow in the volcanic soil.

Many Buddhists who live in the Himalayan peaks also believe in the idea of Shambhala, but for them it represents another level of consciousness that can only be reached by climbing into the inaccessible parts of yourself and finding the value of peace and contentment within. If you do find this place inside yourself, you are able to meet all the other people who have travelled there, and you are able to move into this state of consciousness at will. Although it may only be a mental level it is very real, and it is believed that all of man's collective knowledge and wisdom makes up Shambhala. It makes sense. If you have overcome all your fears, anger and selfishness, you will not only feel pretty good but in your meditations you could travel to some very beautiful places full of light and wisdom, because you have reached that level of sensitivity. Even if the place exists in a physical world it seems that you have to be able to overcome all your limitations before you can reach it. Therefore, if you are the type of person who has to have a physical journey in order to overcome your limitations, start packing and travel in any direction the fancy takes you. Eventually, you will arrive at your own Shambhala which may be the lost valley or it may be a feeling of contentment so that everywhere you are is your Shangri-La.

Shambhala exists at some level and, whether it is physical, mental, spiritual, or a combination of the three, it doesn't really matter. What is important is that you start your journey. You don't need to become religious to start your journey, only a little more sensitive to your needs as opposed to your desires. Try to be more sensitive to those around you, but also make sure that you express yourself and do not suppress what you really feel. It is important to start your journey and carry on with the struggles within yourself even though your ego or your circumstances seem to be as high as the Himalayas. Somewhere inside you there is that valley of peace and wisdom and the only way you'll find it is by becoming sensitive to who and what you are, and facing up to the challenges, disappointments and fears that make up your journey through your earth life.

Vampires

There are many legends about vampires and many films have been made about their lurid exploits as night-wandering, blood-sucking ghosts or dead people return-ing from the grave with the one intention of sucking the blood of sleeping people and causing their death. It is reputed that the vampire keeps alive by sucking fresh blood. Recently, research has shown that blood contains a very high proportion of iron which actually keeps people alive! As legend has it, however, once the creature has bitten you then you, also, become a vampire and so the cycle continues. *Frankenstein* by Mary Shelley has bolstered the vampire image, although the general concept of vampirism is widespread, particularly in Russia and south-eastern Europe. Bodies of vampires are supposed not to decompose after burial but remain in a life-like state and, if the flesh is pierced, blood flows just as it would if they were living. The best way to make sure a vampire is really dead, according to legend, is to behead the body or take out the heart. Alternatively, drive a stake through the heart and a nail through the temples. The stake should be either whitethorn or aspen. In the last resort, the body should be burnt. Legend also has it that carrying garlic on your person will immunize you from attack. Most westerners have found that, when they eat garlic, few people will approach them!

Visualization

Visualization is very important indeed if you want to develop your ESP. Some people are very much better at it than others so try this test and see how well you do. Look hard at a picture, say for about a minute, and then close your eyes and try to reproduce it exactly as you saw it. If you cannot see it exactly practise it again and again and again until you can. After you can do this, develop the mind to create a picture for yourself as if you were painting it. Decide what you want in it and simply put it there, making sure the colours and the form and the texture are just right. The ability to see colours is also important. I have found that many people gain a great deal from using decals, those little circular rainbow ones, on their windows or even in the car. By looking at each colour in turn you will be able to visualize the colour with your eyes shut. The stronger you work at this, the easier everything becomes. Like most things, visualization is an art and needs to be practised. Opening this sense within you means that you will be able to create better affirmations and that your thought-forms will take on a new crispness and clearer definition. Visualizing the body as slimmer or fitter is as invaluable as visualizing someone well and whole who is sick. Visualization comes into all spiritual work so sharpen yours up right now.

Voodoo

Voodoo is usually connected with black magic and various witchcraft practices – all of which are particularly nasty and destructive. To be more precise, the word 'voodoo' represents a religious magical system which has its centre in Haiti, and which was brought there from West Africa by the slaves in the seventeenth and eighteenth centuries. It is also referred to as 'Vodun' and gods of Vodun are a complex lot – a mixture of sacred divinities and supernatural entities who are called upon by the sorcerers or priests to help them with their practice of black magic, spells and much jinxing and hexing.

The main feature of the voodoo ritual is possession of the sorcerer or priest and priestess by these spirits to whom they devote their life. They work themselves into a trance state through long periods of strenuous dancing and chanting and, as the spirit takes them over, they change completely, both physically and in character. It is, essentially, a magical cult, and those who study it believe that the voodoo serpent, an enormous monster, is in charge of all the power in the world and is the master and owner of all the secrets of nature.

Various films and television programmes have been made about the more sensational, magical practices of the voodoo; in films, nothing seems to go right. In the film 'The Possession of Joel Delaney' in the 1970s, the actor playing Joel, the cameraman and the director, all became possessed and had to be exorcised before the film could be finished. Again, it is the belief in such things that gives the power and, if you have no fear in yourself, then you cannot be affected by such practices of magic.

Witchcraft

A witch is a practitioner of witchcraft, the ancient, pre-Christian, occult religion which, in Europe, was called wicca, an Anglo-Saxon word meaning 'the craft of the wise'. The 'witch' has had a bad press over the centuries and immediately conjures up thoughts of devilish things in the New Forest or tales in Salem in the USA. Witches, according to legend, were often served by familiars – imps or demons in the form of cats, dogs, rats or toads. Familiars helped in casting spells or carrying messages. It was believed that the witch nourished and rewarded her familiar with her own blood or milk (and the spot from which the familiar took such nourishment was called a 'witch's mark'). This mark was totally insensitive to pain. During the witch-hunts of the sixteenth century, many were condemned by such a mark or protuberance. Did they ride on broomsticks? Many claimed so, especially during the sixteenth and seventeenth-century witch trials. Was this astral projection under hallucinogens?

Every witch had a cauldron bubbling on the fire and brewed up potions – for love and healing as well as deadly poisons from herbs and barks. Enchanted potions and ointments were her stock-in-trade. Often human hair and finger-nail parings were included. Witch-hunting used to be a great business and was very profitable because the witch's property either went to the Church or to the local landowner.

Wicca is often called the old religion and is not to be confused with black magic which is not a religion but a manipulative art.

Witchcraft, as in any religion, accepts that there is a God or supreme Creator and that, from the supreme Creator, comes life. By the processes of many incarnations we are drawn back into that life. Religious meetings are called Sabbats. Witches do not necessarily fornicate with the Devil, nor are they found promiscuously running half-naked under the light of the moon making weird noises with wode painted on their bodies.

Magic, however, is something that witches know about and religious rites of the Great Sabbats take place four times a year, on 1 February, the last day of April, the first evening in August and the last night of October, Halloween.

Coven is an Anglo-Saxon word from which convent or cevent is derived and simply means a gathering of a witchcraft group, usually composed of thirteen members. Witchcraft ceremonies are related to the moon cycles and there are thirteen moons or lunar months in each year. The Sabbat and Esbat are other names. Often it's thought that the tarot, consisting of thirteen cards, is symbolic of the coven. There are 8000 initiated witches in Britain alone and large numbers in Germany and Australia. The High Priestess is often a spiritual leader and this is the only religion that encourages women to lead. It is important to note that, in America, there are as many as fifty times as many pseudo witches as anywhere in the world. Witches and witchcraft seem to be having a revival recently, probably because orthodox religions seem to be declining, so cults and ancient forms of knowledge take on more importance.

It is important to differentiate between witchcraft and black magic; the old craft of wicca worships the ancient gods, co-operates with nature and the elemental kingdoms and works for good by healing and prayer. Most witches meditate. They are also healers and although stirring up strange ingredients in a cauldron may not be today's practice they do know a great deal about herbs, potions and ointments. Health and well-being is all important. Witches also make spells and charms which are mostly done through positive thinking to create a positive response. Timing is of great importance here for even the hours of the day have a particular meaning. Midnight is not called the witching hour for nothing as the influences then are quieter and calmer, but I am told that, from midnight until dawn, is the most potent time of all. During the witch-hunting Middle Ages, when the witches prospered through the sales of love potions, herbs and counselling advice, covens went underground and only in the more isolated parts of Britain such as Suffolk, north Staffordshire and Hampshire did they thrive. Only in this century have the witchcraft laws been taken off the statutory books of Great Britain. Riding broomsticks and meeting with the devil lover called Satan is a far cry from the old religion. A true witch will not debase the art she has been taught.

Here is an ancient love spell:

Make a little heart out of red flannel or cloth. Pierce it with three brand new needles. Throw it into the fire saying:

'It is not the heart of my love I mean to burn
But the head of my true love I mean to turn.'

And the best of luck!

Wraith

This is not a ghost but a projection of someone who is alive to some other person. This usually happens in deep natural sleep but can be done during the day at will. Legend has it that wraiths are generally supposed to foretell the death of the person who is seen and it is probably the approach of death that weakens the link between physical and spiritual bodies. Even when death may be violent or accidental, wraiths can appear as it is certain that the astral or spiritual body will know this!

Yin and Yang

These are the prime passive and active principles of the universe. Yin is the female principle and is the negative force, while Yang is the male principle and the positive force. The forces are always both contrasting and yet completing each other, and are often described as heaven and hell, man and woman, good and evil, black and white, great and small, hard and soft, odd and even, life and death, and love and hate. Between them they cover all of existence and all types of relating. Yin and Yang make up the doctrine of Taoism, and the interpretation of any possible Yin-Yang experience may be worked out through the *I Ching*. Acupuncture and acupressure treatments are based on vital energy, or Chi, which manifests through the positive and negative in Yin and Yang; disease is seen as an imbalance of this energy. Macrobiotics also show which foods are Yang and which are Yin and again illness can result from an imbalance of one type or another.

Zombie

A Zombie was originally a god among the African tribes around the Congo but, more recently, the term has become part of voodoo magic in the West Indies. In voodoo West African magic, the zombie is the deity of the python as it is in Haiti, the centre of the voodoo cult. It is also regarded as a magical power that can enter into, and reanimate, a dead body. When this happens the person becomes more or less like a robot and is controlled by the voodoo sorcerer or priest, doing exactly as he is told.

This word is in everyday use today, particularly in American slang, and applies to someone who looks different or strange in appearance, mind or action, and somehow has the appearance of being more dead then alive.

Zombie means 'living dead'. It is said that sorcerers and magicians have the ability to restore the life of a corpse by allowing some of the spirit to re-enter the body for a short period of time. This means they have control of the body and are able to manipulate it through drugs to keep it permanently in a semi-concious state. Without any will of their own, they live an almost animal-like existence, obeying the sorcerer's will. Often a dead person is killed a second time to stop the would-be sorcerer's intention. This even happens today.

Other Arrow Books of interest:

THE HANDBOOK OF CHINESE HOROSCOPES

Theodora Lau

Are you a sentimental but crafty Rat, a serious and dutiful Ox, or a captivating but unpredictable Tiger? Here, in the most comprehensive book ever written on Chinese astrology, you can find out which of the twelve animal signs of the lunar calendar is yours, how your sign is affected by the Yin and Yang, how your Moon sign and your Sun sign affect each other – and which of the other animal signs you're compatible with.

THE BOOK OF CHINESE BELIEFS

Frena Bloomfield

Earth magic, ghost weddings, passports to the after-life: the spirit world of the Chinese exists side-by-side with everyday reality, and affects every aspect of Chinese life from diet and decor to getting married or opening a business.

Frena Bloomfield has lived and worked in Hong Kong and has talked in depth to many practitioners of the magic arts. *The Book of Chinese Beliefs* is a fascinating introduction to a rich culture where the dead are ever-present and even the siting of a house or village is governed by the laws of earth magic.